Real Life Adventures

GM Matheny

True Christian Short
Stories for Your Edification
and Enjoyment!

Author Garry and wife, Nancy

G. M. Matheny was a navy diver on the nuclear submarine USS *Halibut* SSN 587 and received the Legion of Merit for a special operation. He graduated from Pacific Coast Baptist Bible College in 1979 and has authored five books. He and his wife, Nancy, were called to the mission field, and they've served as missionaries in Romania since 1991.

Of the short stories that follow, a few of them will not be considered "adventures", but they are all true, from a US Navy diver in Soviet territorial waters to being on a train with six small children in Europe. Some are funny or serious but all are helpful for our Christian walk. Adults and young people enjoy these and parents may find it helpful to read them to their children.

Table of Contents

ADVENTURE #1
The Matheny Family Express

On the train with
our six young
children in Europe.

Getting to the Mission Field - a true story. I wanted to call this adventure "Murder on the Orient Express" after Agatha Christie's book, but it's not a "Who done it?" It's a "Why did I do it?" Sometimes spiritual truths are best learned on life's path. We left Seattle, Washington, on April 29, 1991, and crossed the Romanian border on May 6 that year. Besides flying on two airplanes, we boarded five trains in seven days, and the main one was the Orient Express out of Paris to Budapest, Hungary.

We were on our way to the mission field! This was not a survey trip, where you check out the field to make sure it's the Lord's calling. I knew the Lord wanted us in Romania, so we just went. "We" included my wife, Nancy, and our six children: Ben was the oldest at eleven; Philip, nine; Bethe, seven; Ruth, five; Sarah, two and a half; and Caleb, who was just six weeks old. The Bible says, *"Happy is the man that hath his quiver full of them [children]"* (Ps. 127:5). My wife likes to respond, "Yes, dear, happy is the *man*!

Our family a few months before we left for Romania. Benjamin at the top, then Philip, Bethe, Ruthe and Sarah. Nancy was pregnant with Caleb.

We had flown from the Seattle-Tacoma International Airport, in Washington State, to the John F. Kennedy Airport in New York, and then on to Lisbon, Portugal. The reason we didn't fly straight to Romania was because the travel agent said we would save a thousand dollars by taking the train. She also told us it would be a great opportunity to tour Europe on the way there. It may sound like fun being in cities like Madrid or Paris, but the only thing we saw was the inside of train stations. Trains are not all that fun or romantic with twenty-one pieces of luggage and six small children. I was afraid of losing our kids everywhere we went. Nancy was also still recovering from Caleb's birth, which required a cesarean section.

When our flight landed in Lisbon, we needed to get a room, as we had several hours to wait before our first train would leave. At the hotel, we were shown an overpriced apartment with only one room for all eight of us. When I complained about the price, the owner showed me a smaller room with five mattresses on the floor for only slightly less. I'm sure it was a room the hotel kept to make all us gullible tourists think we were getting a bargain by taking the more expensive room. So we paid for the more expensive room. At least it had a bathroom, and we needed to get some sleep. We were beat from the trip and the jet lag. Later that evening, we squeezed everyone into two taxis (no small trick with all that luggage), and off we went to the train station to confirm our tickets.

That's when I started having language problems. I just assumed I would always find someone like the man at the hotel who could speak English, and if not, I thought I would just speak "loud and slow." Well, of course, that doesn't work, but I automatically started doing this every time someone started talking to me in a foreign language. From then on, we did a lot of Pictionary and pantomime, especially on the trains. Fortunately, the word for *toilet* in most countries is similar to the English word, which helps, because with six small children, you are always looking for one.

At any rate, we boarded the train. But you have to get to train stations early to get all the tickets in the same car, especially when you have busy trains and eight tickets. Well, I was not early enough. This meant that the first night, my children were all strewn up and down the train in different train cars. Seriously! I begged some people to let three of my children in one compartment. They kindly made room so they could be near Nancy and the babies in the next compartment. Each compartment had overhead shelves for baggage, with either six or eight seats. I could not get a seat close to my family, so that first night, to keep from getting our luggage stolen, I slept in the hall *on top of our luggage* which was on the floor. I was told I was very lucky that the train personnel allowed me to do that, as the halls in trains are quite narrow. Actually, I still had a good attitude, because at that point I was all gung-ho about going to the mission field.

The next morning we pulled into Madrid. I had first-class tickets, but everywhere I went, I needed to check in and get seat reservations, and as I already explained, this was a problem. In the main terminal in Madrid, I managed to waste most of our time in the wrong line! I finally got my seat tickets with barely enough time to catch the next train. The train was, as I remember, twenty-one tracks down from our previous train. And with little time we had to do this (about 10 min.) it was a big problem. Fortunately, Ben was big enough to help me with the luggage, and Philip was able to help with his sisters while Nancy handled the two little ones. We had to run back and forth several times to get the luggage.

Once in line to board, I started asking if it

was the right train. I didn't want to get on the wrong train like I had waited in the wrong line to get tickets. The first person I asked did not know any English but looked at my ticket and pointed me toward the train. The next person spoke a little English and also pointed me to the train. So, I felt confident that it was the correct train and got all my family boarded, with our twenty-one pieces of luggage. This train car was open inside, with no separate compartments and had around sixty seats in it. I settled my family in some seats and breathed a sigh of relief that we had made it in time. For some reason, I thought I ought to ask just one more time if we were on the right train. So I said out loud, "Does anyone here speak English?"

"I do," said the man across the aisle.

"Oh good," I said. I showed him our tickets and asked, "This train goes to Paris, right?"

"No, it doesn't," he said.

"Yes, it does!" I insisted.

"No, it doesn't," he told me again.

"Hey, other people told me it does."

"I'm sorry, but it does not go to Paris," he said confidently.

"Well, what train does?" I asked. He

pointed to the front of the train car and said, "That train does."

I was confused by the direction he was pointing and told him, "That train is this train!" By pointing to the front of the car it was still the same train. I couldn't figure out what he meant.

"Come here," he said, and I followed him outside. He pointed to the same train we had been on and said, "It's true that this train goes to Paris, but this car you're on does not." He then said, "Look, they're uncoupling your car right now from the rest of the train, and you only have one minute to get your family off and onto the next car."

"Bother!" Somehow, we did this, luggage and all. The whole family got situated into one small compartment with eight seats and two other people in it. We had to place some of our luggage out in the hall, but we were finally settled. Nancy was a trooper, but we were clearly both exhausted from this European "tour." We had gone a few miles outside of Madrid when Nancy leaned over to me and said, "Next time, let's fly."

I told her, "Yeah, I have been thinking the same thing but didn't want to say anything."

The only thing I remember about that part of the trip was seeing small towns that reminded me of Mexico, and one train station even looked like something out of a cowboy-western film. That part of Spain just did not resemble what I thought Europe would look like. We also spent one long night in the train on our way to Paris. In no train on our trip did we have beds to sleep in (or none I could afford). We just stayed in our seats the whole way. *"Not fun!"*

The next morning, we arrived in Paris and had a long wait in the train station for our next train, the Orient Express. We spent almost six hours sitting on the cement floor. I couldn't find any hotel that would let me put my whole family into one apartment, and the prices were too high to get two rooms. Looking back, I was just too stingy with our money and should have paid for the rooms, even if they were overpriced. Later that afternoon I found one hotel that would let me put all my family into one apartment, and with less than three hours, we tried to get some sleep. At least we could use the shower.

The Orient Express was the longest leg of our trip and was to take us through parts of four countries. When the train left that evening, I managed to get my family into one compartment with no one else, plus all our luggage. Because we were at the train station early enough, I could get our seats reserved, but only until we entered Germany that night. But I was told at that time it was unlikely the train would be crowded.

We filled the center aisle between the facing seats with some of our bags and tried to make a place where we could sleep, smelly diapers and all. Nancy had run out of Pampers and was using cloth diapers, washing them out in the train's restroom and then hanging them out to dry in our compartment. Well, it wasn't the Marriott, but at least we were all together.

We did not sleep for long before we were awakened. The train was somewhere in Germany and it was about 1:30 a.m. The door opened, the light came on, and an elderly couple stood there staring at us. And then the lady said, in loud, broken English, four words that you never want to hear while traveling: "Those seats are ours!"

I wiped the sleep from my eyes and looked at her for a couple of seconds and then got up on one knee. "Well it's going to be crowded with all of us here and all this luggage. Maybe you could find another place," I suggested. Obviously, I didn't want to get my family up and move the luggage.

That's when she hollered, real loud, "Get the conductor! Get the conductor! Get the conductor!"

I said, "Ma'am, it's all right. We'll move."

She surprised and irritated me with her loud voice and definitely woke me up. I stumbled over the luggage and out of the compartment into the hall. I thought maybe I could just find an empty compartment, and she would be satisfied with that. Surprisingly, the compartment right next to ours was completely empty.

"Oh, look, the compartment right here is empty," I said.

She started hollering again, "Get the conductor!" And she kept repeating it like a mantra.

I shot back, "Okay, lady, we're out of here!"

I'm sorry, but she made me upset. Our two youngest were crying, and I was trying to move my family and all that luggage in the middle of the night. While I was doing this, I prayed a little prayer and said, "Well, Lord, what do you think about this?" Guess what verse came to my mind? *"Blessed are they who throw loud mouths off of trains.*" No, actually the verse God gave me was, *"Whosoever shall compel thee to go a mile, go with him twain."* I said, "Okay." I turned around, thinking, "How could I apply this verse on a train?" This elderly couple had two little carry-on bags and two big military-style duffel bags. They were each about 70 years old or older, and it would have been difficult to lift the duffel bags over their heads and put them on the shelf where they belonged. They couldn't just place their luggage between the seats (as we had done) because there would be no room for their feet or the other people who might come into the compartment later.

At any rate, I stepped over and grabbed her duffel bag. Her eyes bugged out, and she *slapped my hands*! She said, "Get your hands off those bags. They belong to us." And she reached out and pulled back the bag.

I said, "Hey, I'm not stealing them. I'm going to put them on the shelf for you."

She said, "What?" She couldn't understand why I would do that, and I did not feel like trying to explain it to her. So I just reached down and grabbed the bag and stepped inside the compartment and somehow managed to lift it over my head onto the shelf. It was very heavy! They must have had books in those bags.

I was thinking how fortunate they were that I was there. I stepped out into the hall again to get the other bag. This time, she put both of her hands on it and said, "No, you can't have it."

I stood up and looked at her and said, "Hey, I'm not stealing it!"

"I know," she said.

"You know?"

"Yes," she responded.

"Well, what's the problem?"

"It's not right that you should do this," she said sheepishly.

"It's not?" I said.

"No, it's not."

They both had guilty looks on their faces. And I couldn't help but laugh. Now I was feeling *glad* because they were feeling *bad*. I said, "No, I want to do this." So I grabbed the other bag and put it on the shelf. I rubbed it in a little by taking the two small handbags and putting them on the seats next to the windows where they were going to sit. I then said, "If you need anything at all, we're right next to you. Just knock on the wall here, and I will come right over and help you."

They were really feeling bad, and both of them waved their hands at me to just go away. I said, "Seriously, if I can help you at all, I really would like to."

"Yes, yes, just go," she said and pushed me away. During this whole time, her husband did not talk at all. As it turned out, he could not speak English.

I went to the compartment right next door and told Nancy what had happened and how I had all this joy. But she said, "I'm still upset with them!" She was trying to get the babies back to sleep.

You won't believe what happened next.

That same night, four hours later, about 5:30 a.m. in our new compartment, the door opened again, the light came on again, and again there were two people standing there, and they said those same four words: "Those are our seats!"

I got up on one knee and just stared at them, thinking, "You can't reason with these people." While I was looking at them, I noticed my wife had gotten up also. I turned toward her, and her face was very close to mine, uncomfortably close, and she had these snake eyes with a look that said, "I'm not moving!" I looked at her and I looked at the people who were standing at the door, and I wondered, "How do I get myself into these situations?"

God sends help from an unexpected source.

The couple who had kicked us out earlier that night apparently had never gone to sleep. They were still all dressed up, and they came over and started asking this new couple what they were doing. I don't know what country we were in, being on a moving train, but both couples knew some English, which became their language of conversation. The lady who forced us to move earlier started raising her voice at the other couple. (She was really good at that!) "This is a very nice family we have here," referring to us. "What, can't you see they have six little children?" She did all the talking, while her husband and I just nodded in agreement. Then she said, "Surely you could have found some place else to sit?" And she added, "Why, what kind of people are you, anyway?" She was great! And the new couple left! She then turned to me and said the same thing I had said to her, "We're right next door, and if you need anything at all, you just knock, and we will come right over and help you."

All I could manage to say was, "Okay." The next day we made some new friends, as they shared their lunch with us. Isn't the Word of God powerful? If I had not obeyed that verse, I would still be upset with her, but instead, I had and still have a smile about it.

The train left without me!

Later that day our train pulled into Vienna, Austria. I left Nancy and the kids on the train and went to find something to make sandwiches for lunch. I knew I did not have much time before our train left, and I had planned it so that I should have returned in time. But when I came back, the train was gone!

I thought maybe I was confused, and the train was on another track. I looked, but to no avail. I was in a panic! *Where will my family go? All the way to Budapest, or will they get off at the next stop and wait for me?* I could imagine what must have been going through my wife's mind as the train pulled out of the station without me.

I showed my tickets to a conductor, he motioned with his hands for me to follow him. Our train *had* been moved to another track, to hook up with a different engine. What a relief!

Once inside, Nancy and I agreed it would be better not to step off the train at the rest of the stops until we arrived in Budapest, which would be that evening. If we needed more food, we would just buy some chips or soda on the train.

That day, for the first time, I started to enjoy the trip. We had enough food and wouldn't have to get off the train until the evening. Everything looked clean and neat in the cities we were passing through. The houses were pretty, there were neat rows of flowers, and I remember seeing this well-to-do couple riding their horses.

I mean no offense to the people who live in Eastern Europe, but back in 1991, trying to compare it to the West would have been like trying to compare night to day. Crossing over into what used to be called the Iron Curtain countries was a real eye-opener. We crossed at Hungary and the differences were immediately visible. All the buildings were run-down, and the signs and towns looked like they had not been painted since World War II. Signs were so dirty you could barely read them, and the unattractive houses were painted a brownish-orange. Mind you, it is different today, but then the whole country looked drab.

When we pulled into Budapest that evening, the train station was dark and dingy. I had to get our baggage off and try to find some rooms for three nights. Though today it is different, back then we needed to get visas to enter Romania. We had to wait until the Romanian Embassy opened on Monday, otherwise the trip could have been at least two days shorter. It had been three and a half days since we boarded the first train in Portugal, not to mention the flights from Seattle and New York. We were all tired and wishing the trip was over, and it was then that I started asking the Lord, "Just get us to Romania."

We ended up with all my family and luggage in two taxis, and we drove around Budapest looking for a place to spend the night. The taxi driver told us the first hotel we went to was a good place, but it did not look so good to me, just old. I asked for a room, and the man at the counter told me it would be $250 a night!

"There must be some mistake. We don't need a fancy suite, just one room will do."

"It is one room," he replied.

"One room?" I asked in disbelief.

"Yes, one room, one bed, one night," he responded. I turned around and walked out!

When I walked outside, I was struck by the fact that on both sides of the street, as far as I could see, cars were parked with no openings left, and both of our taxis were double-parked. The taxi driver explained that most of the cars were from Romania because the people were leaving Romania and trying to go to the West. Therefore all the cheap rooms had already been taken.

He then took us to an old, run-down apartment complex. There was no sidewalk, just mud. He said he had a friend there who sometimes rented out his apartment. The hallway leading to the apartment was poorly lit, and I was starting to wonder if I had made a mistake. I have a good imagination, and I was wondering if I was going to get hit over the head. His friend wasn't home, and I was glad to get out of there.

When we got back to the taxis, Nancy said, "We need to do something." My family was crammed into these two taxis, with bags on top of the taxis, bags in the trunks, and bags on the seats.

I prayed again, "Lord, just get us to Romania," and I told my wife, "Yeah, we'll do something." I asked the taxi driver if he knew of anything better, and he said,

"Do you want to try a hotel service?" I didn't know what he was talking about, but with the meters on both of these taxis still running, I said,

"Yeah, sure. Let's try it." We pulled up to a well-lit curb near the center of town. And out came these people with photo albums filled with pictures of rooms for rent. I said to the taxi driver, "These don't look like hotel rooms."

"They're not," he said. He explained that people who rented out rooms in their houses would bring pictures to this agency, and the agency would rent the rooms for them. We ended up renting one room for $100 a night in some guy's house. We spent the next three days there, while the owner slept in the kitchen. This was really different, but it seemed to work, and we were out of options.

On Monday morning, we picked up our visas from the Romanian Embassy. We had written to a Romanian man who was setting up an apartment for us to rent in a town called Oradea, which was just inside the border of Romania. After my fourth try from a telephone booth in Budapest, I was able to get through to him to let him know we were on our way. After I received my tickets from the train station, I thought, "This will be our last changing of trains."

The last thing I remember about Hungary was the McDonald's that was in this dark and dingy train station. McDonald's, with all its lively colors, seemed so out of place there. My family was "safe" on the train, so I thought I would buy something familiar, Big Macs and Cokes. There were no McDonald's in Romania at that time (and would not be for six more years), so we were in a sense saying good-bye to civilization.

I thought, "We've made it; I'll never have to do this again." I had been waiting for twelve years after graduating from Bible college to set foot on the mission field. Just one more hurdle awaited us.

We were two hours out of Budapest on what I thought was our last leg of the train ride. And then our train stopped in the middle of nowhere. The station was small and no town was in sight; there were not even many houses around. The loudspeakers at the station started blaring something in Hungarian. Normally, I couldn't have cared less. I had our tickets, we were on the right train, and it was to take us all the way to Romania. But it seemed like everyone was getting off the train. I told Nancy I had checked the train car in front and behind ours, and they were empty except for us. The train ride was supposed to be about five hours, so I knew we were not in Romania yet. I said what seemed obvious, "I think we are the only ones on the train."

My wife pulled back the curtain and looked outside and said, "I don't see how. There is no one around here. It's just a farming community." That's when somebody in a train uniform, who seemed to be in charge, knocked on the window across the narrow hall from our compartment. I walked over to the window and let it down. He knew two English words: "Off, you!" I showed him our tickets and told him we were on our way to Romania and that I *just knew* this was the right train.

I'm sure he understood the tickets, but I doubt he understood me, and he just responded with, "You, off!" I tried to explain again but he was even louder. "Off, you!" I didn't want to get off. What was I to do in the middle of nowhere with my family and all this luggage? He laughed to himself, and went and found some baggage people who came onto our train. They opened the windows and literally started throwing our luggage *out the windows onto the adjacent train track!* So, we got *off* the train.

Picture this: We were standing on the tracks of an old train station, with our twenty-one pieces of luggage, six children, and the station's loudspeakers still blaring. I felt like I was getting ready to go to a concentration camp. My daughter Bethe, who was carrying this huge stuffed white rabbit (It was as big as she was and looked ridiculous. We had bought it for her in the States.), walked up to me with a worried look on her face, pulled on my pant leg, and said, "Dad, what are we doing here?"

"I don't know," I responded. Not a good position for a daddy, who is supposed to have all the answers. But I didn't have to wait long.

The man who threw our baggage out came with some carts, loaded up our luggage, and put our children on top, motioning to us to follow him. He led us around to the back of the train station, where there were six blue buses. The people on the buses were all upset because they had been waiting on us, but how were we to know, not being able to understand what the loudspeakers had said. The men loaded our luggage onto the last bus. Nancy stood in front with Caleb, who was crying, and I stood next to the door in the back, with our luggage literally against my face. Our children were placed on different seats or on luggage that was in the aisle.

Sometimes on this trip, and especially then, I noticed our children looking at us with an expression that said, "Is this okay? Is everything going to be all right?" Of course, as a parent you never let on any concerns you might have, and you just keep your best face on.

Personally, I was in an awkward position on this bus, because if the back doors opened, our luggage would fall out and I would be pushed onto the street. All the buses went about ten miles down the road to another train station, where everyone got off. When the doors opened in the back, sure enough, I fell out with some of our baggage. To this day, I do not know why we had to take those buses. Perhaps some repairs were being made on the train track, but we never encountered anyone who could explain to us, in English, what the reason was.

The next train we boarded was even smaller and much older□. It looked like a train from World War II. We knew we were going to be overcrowded. I told my wife to just get on the last car and find a place for our children, while Benjamin and I moved the luggage to the train. Nancy found a compartment where she and our other five children could sit with two other families. It was cramped, to say the least, and there was no room for our luggage. Benjamin and I stayed at the far end of the train car with our luggage on the floor in the hallway. The halls in the trains are narrow, and this hall was filled with people because there was no place left to sit, which meant that people were now standing on our luggage! I gritted my teeth and asked the Lord one more time: "Just get us to Romania."

We stood for the rest of the trip and watched people smash our bags. When we finally came to the border, the train made a long, slow stop, and you could actually feel each train car hitting the car in front of it, bang, bang, bang, bang, about ten times. I asked some men who were standing on our bags, "Is this the border? Are we at Romania?"

A man next to us nodded yes and pointed to

the front of the train and said, "Romania, Romania."

I looked out the window in the direction he was pointing. I had never been in Eastern Europe before, much less Romania, but less than a mile away was the country I had been dreaming to get to. My first thought was, "It doesn't look any different than Hungary."

I noticed there were a lot of military people at the train station, who looked like they worked there. We crossed the frontier of Romania on May 6, 1991, about a year and four months after their revolution. During the revolution, many people had died, and they were working hard to make their transition to a Western economy. It is amazing to me how much the country has been transformed in the last 28 years. There are large stores now, and one can buy anything he wants, but back then one had to wait five hours inline just to buy bread! Now conditions are much better and Romania has joined both NATO and the European Community. But in May of 1991, America was like Disneyland compared to Eastern Europe.

We waited on the train for a while, then three young soldiers boarded with machine guns.

These were not draped over their shoulders, but in their hands. One of them hollered, "Pasaporte, pasaporte." I could at least figure out what that meant, and I handed him all of our passports. He stared at me and said, "Opt Pasaporte?" He then put his machine gun under his arm and lifted up eight fingers. I nodded yes and eventually he understood that the rest of my family was up front in a compartment. He then turned around and walked off the train with our passports. I had been told to never let anyone walk off with your passports, as they're the only acceptable proof of who you are. So I followed him off the train and tried to get my passports back. Two more soldiers came up with machine guns and pushed me back up against the train! (This literally happed.) Well, you can't argue with people holding machine guns. I must have had a startled look on my face, as one solider said, "OK, OK, no worry. Go on train."

I got back on the train and thought, "They have my passports, and if this train leaves, I'm sunk."

After about ten minutes, a uniformed customs agent came on and said something to me in Romanian. I shrugged my shoulders and said,

"I don't understand." To my surprise he started speaking to me in broken English.

"Are these your bags?" he pointed to our bags that were on the ground in the hallway.

"Well, yes, they are," I said, and added, "I'm sorry, but there is no place to put them."

"Where is your paperwork?"

"For what?" I asked.

"For your bags. Show me the papers for your bags."

I told him we had been in several countries and no one had asked for papers before. Apparently, these papers were to contain a list of what was in each bag. He was, after all, a customs agent, and his job was to inspect what was brought into the country. "You have no papers, you open bags," he said. He moved people off and away from our bags and started opening them. Some of our "bags" were only cardboard boxes with masking tape on them, so he used his knife to cut the tape.

Then something happened that I will never forget. One of our cardboard boxes was filled with Romanian New Testaments, and it also contained my English Bible and a Russian Bible that someone had given me while I was in

Hungary, who had told me to give it to the Russians who come into Romania to sell things at the open-air market. This customs agent only wanted to know one thing: "Why you have Bibles?" I knew it had been illegal to bring in Bibles under Communist rule, but since Romania's revolution, I was told it was no longer a concern. I couldn't understand what the problem was, but he was not going to let this pass. He started firing off questions. "Why you have Bibles? Are you going to sell them? Why you in our country? How long you going to stay? What you going to do?" He had lots of questions.

"I'm not going to sell them," I said.

"Why you have them?"

"I'm just going to give them away."

I was afraid to tell him I was a Baptist preacher coming to start churches. If he didn't like the Bibles, then for sure he wouldn't like my being a missionary. This man seemed to have the authority not only to make the train wait, but also to approve what and who went into Romania (or stayed behind). And then, surprisingly, he asked, "You Romanian?"

"Romanian? No, I'm American."

"You no Romanian?" he said

again.

I shook my head and said, "No, I'm American."

"You American?"

"Yes," I said.

"You American citizen?" He asked.

"Yes, I'm an American citizen."

"No!" he said, and he started going through the box of Bibles.

I stared at him for a moment and then said to him, "What do you mean, 'No?'"

"No! You no American citizen!"

I said, "What, is this a joke?"

Then he found the Russian Bible I had. "This is Russian Bible," he said, and he seemed quite proud of himself for finding it. "Why you have Russian Bible?"

"I'm just going to give it away," I said.

He looked at its pages for a few seconds and asked, "You Russian?"

I said "No!" and reached in my pocket for my passport to prove who I was. But, of course, it wasn't there; the soldiers had taken them earlier. I thought, "What are they trying to pull here?" I put my hand in the air as though I was taking an oath and said, "I'm an American citizen!" It now seems funny to me, but at the time it certainly was not.

"You American?"

"Yes, American!" I responded.

"You an American citizen?"

"Yes, you got it. An American citizen!"

"No," he said.

"No what?" I shot back.

"No, you not an American citizen!"

I was totally bewildered by it. And then I said, "Okay, I'm not an American, I'm not Russian, and I'm not Romanian. Who am I?"

He reached for my English Bible, which was also in the cardboard box, and said, "Read this." I thought he wanted to see if I could read English, to prove if I was an American. I started to read the first verse I saw, but he stopped me and said, "No, read this." He pointed to Ephesians 2:19, the verse that talks about Christians being citizens of Heaven. He stopped me at that point and said, "You Christian, and Christians are citizens of Heaven."

I stared at him and said "Yeah," questioning where this was going to lead. It seemed to have helped me to have read even that one verse in God's Word, something I needed, because I had this crazy thought I might actually be going to jail.

He then looked both ways and said, "I am Christian also, and I also citizen of Heaven." He then reached for my hand and shook it and said, "I am so glad you come to our country!"

I had mixed feelings at this point. He was a Christian and I was not in trouble, but he had really pulled one on me and all I could do was grin. He told me that before the revolution, he would let Bibles enter Romania. He said one man had written a book about him, which said, "God had blinded the eyes of the customs agent." He told me when he opened bags during Communism and saw any Bibles, he just closed the bags back up and said nothing. He added, "God didn't blind my eyes. He just put me here to let Bibles through."

I was glad that was over. Our bags had been inspected, and everything was a "go" for getting into Romania. After a few more minutes the soldiers came back with our passports. As I understand it, they just registered them there at the border. The train started moving again, and we passed over into Romania. I was relieved to have all that behind me, and glad to know we were getting off at the first city. When the train stopped for the last leg of our seven-day ordeal, I realized the Lord had answered my prayer, "Just get us to Romania." As planned, a man named Radu met us. I knew him only through correspondence and the one phone call I had made from Budapest, but he was very helpful. He had hired two taxis to take our belongings and family to an apartment, where the refrigerator was full of food—something that was hard to do then. It was then that I got my first taste of Romanian bread, which is better than American bread.

Radu did not stay long. "You must be tired," he said, and he handed me the key to the apartment and left.

There was about an hour left of daylight, so I went outside to look around. It was a new world to me. It was common to see a flock of sheep or a couple of cows on side streets. More people walked because fewer people had cars then; some even still used horse-drawn wagons (though not now). To me it was new sights, new sounds, and a little scary. I did not know what to expect—how we would be received, being foreigners. Thankfully, Romanians are a most hospitable people, and there was no need for worry.

By this time, we were all exhausted, so after we ate, we went to bed early. Our two boys slept in the living room, our three girls in one bedroom, our baby in a makeshift crib with Nancy and I in the other bedroom. Everyone went to sleep except for me; I just couldn't sleep. I lay there in bed staring into a dark room for a while, then finally got up and went into the living room, where there was a small light shining from the kitchen. I thought, "I will pray one more time and thank the Lord for getting us here." I knelt down on the living room floor, **but what I prayed surprised me.** I had never even thought to pray this before, but I prayed, "Lord, please let all of our children be missionaries." I thought, "Why did I pray that?" Especially after all we had been through, would I want my children to go through such a time when they are older? The only thing I can tell you is that, even after everything we had suffered on our journey, I had this joy and thankfulness in my heart, and I guess I wanted them to have the same.

Joy like that comes only from the Lord, not from a life (or a train trip) without problems, not from geography (being in your own country with friends and relatives), not from ink on paper (money), but from doing the will of God from the heart.

ADVENTURE #2
"Cheerful Giver"
or
Scrooge buys his wife a ring!

The Bible says we are not to give *"grudgingly or of necessity"* (II Corinthians 9:6), but we are to give cheerfully, for *"God loveth a cheerful giver."*

A man at church once said, "Pastor, the Bible says I'm to give cheerfully."

"That's right," the pastor said.

"Now Pastor, I don't know if you know it or not, but I don't give cheerfully."

The pastor said, "You don't?"

"No, I don't. So, therefore I'm not obeying the Bible when I give my money, am I?" he asked.

"Well, that's right, you're not," the pastor answered.

Then he said, "So, therefore I don't have to give my money anymore!"

"No, that's not what it means. It means you have to ask God to forgive you for your attitude, and then give. It's both—give and give cheerfully."

True story

Nancy and I were visiting a friend's house, and his wife was showing my wife the new ring her husband had bought her. My wife said to me, "Isn't it pretty?"

I was stingy with "my" money and wasn't interested. I replied, "Yeah, it's okay," and I thought that would be the last of it. A few days later we were in a mall, and I couldn't find my wife. I looked around and saw her in one of those corner jewelries shops (the corner shops in malls cost the most to rent, and those who sell jewelry are usually there). Now, I don't need to tell you it got my attention to see her in that store. I walked right up to her and said, "What's the matter?"

"Nothing," she replied, "I was just looking at this ring. Isn't it pretty?"

I was supposed to say, "Oh yeah, that's beautiful," but of course I didn't.

She was looking through the glass at this little ruby ring, and I was looking through the glass at the little price tag next to the ring. It's disgusting how much they want for those little stones! For the same amount of money, I could have bought four new tires for my car. Have you ever thought about the fact that rings don't do anything? I understand a wedding ring—at least it serves the purpose of telling others you're married—but every other ring just sits there on your wife's finger, doing nothing.

"You want to buy that?" I said, rather loudly.

"No, I just thought it was pretty." And she added, "I don't need to buy it, or anything."

"Good. Let's go!"

I got out of there as quickly as I could. I wanted to put some distance between me and that ring. But my wife was not in such a hurry. She was about ten paces behind me and she was moping. When I saw how dejected she looked, I thought, "I've got to buy her a stupid ring. She won't be happy unless I buy her a ring." I spent the next two weeks coming up with some extra money so I could buy her a ring. Oh, I bought it at a pawnshop...

I thought, "Okay, I'm going to get her the ring, but I am going to let her know how I feel about it!"

Did you ever receive something you wanted, but you did not like how it was given to you? Well, that's what happened to Nancy. I came home one evening and she was all sweet, because she knew from the tone of my voice I was not a happy camper. I feel guilty telling you this story, but, well, here is what happened.

I hollered from the front door to find her, "Hey, I'm home. Remember the ring you wanted? Well, here it is." I actually dropped it on the table... She ended up wearing it just to keep peace in the house. The point is that I gave, but not the right way.

Thankfully, I have learned some things. The reason a wife looks at the ring that "sits" on her finger is not to count the monetary value of it, but because it represents a token of her husband's love. But every time Nancy looked at her ring, she probably saw me bouncing it off the table. Ouch!

I'm sorry to say, a few years passed before I realized what I had done. It was while visiting churches on our second furlough that God got a hold of my heart about this. I was driving my car and listening to a cassette tape someone had given me. The entire message was about a preacher buying his wife a ring, and it was forty-five minutes long! I was convicted by it, and I wanted to turn it off, but I thought, "This message doesn't bother me." I must have been driving slowly, because cars were swerving around me and a couple of drivers honked their horns at me.

The preacher went into detail about buying his wife a ring. He talked about how he finally found the right stone, but the setting was wrong, so he actually asked the jeweler if he would take the stone off the ring, and he was even willing to pay him the full price to get it done! I was listening to this and thinking, "Just buy her a ring and get it over with!" This preacher then drove to another state where he remembered seeing a setting he liked.

When the preacher showed the jeweler the stone he had bought in another state and asked him if he would be willing to place the stone on a ring in his store, the jeweler said, "She must be some special lady."

"Yes, she is," the preacher said, and added, "I wanted it to be something special, because she will wear it the rest of her life."

That's when I said out loud, "I'm sorry." I was alone in my car, just me, the cassette, and the Lord, Who was convicting me.

I spent the next six weeks looking for a new ring for my wife, and I hate shopping. My idea of a "good time" of shopping is to see how fast I can find what I want and get out. "Find it, buy it, bag it, and leave." But now I was actually enjoying searching for just the right ring for Nancy. I found what I wanted in five weeks, but I waited another week to give it to her because our anniversary was coming up. It was all I could do to wait that last week. The ring had six little rubies on it as God gave us six children.

Attitude made the difference.

A week before our anniversary, Nancy had pointed to the calendar and said, "Oh look, next week is our anniversary."

"Hum, how about that," I said. She didn't want me to forget, of course, but I thought, "She won't be expecting what I bought her!"

When our anniversary came, she said she wanted to go out for Mexican food, so I took her to Taco Bell.

Someone said, "You took your wife to *Taco Bell* on your anniversary?!"

Anyway, I sat down at our table at the "restaurant" before she did, and I placed the gift on the table across from me.

When she saw the small gift, she said, "This is for me?"

"Yes!" I'm smiling, I'm happy, and she was smiling, not knowing what to expect.

"Oh, you shouldn't have," she said.

"Uh-huh …" I said.

It was funny, because when she unwrapped the box and looked at the ring, she first said, "Wow!" But she kept looking at the ring, and then her expression and voice changed to a more serious one, and she looked at me and said, "Is this real?"

I was laughing and said, "Yes!" It's strange, but giving her the ring made me appreciate her more. The Bible says, *"For where your treasure is, there will be your heart also."*

She then stood up right in front of everybody at Taco Bell and reached across the table, pulled my face toward her, and started kissing me all over my face—with everybody watching! I guess I should take back what I said about rings not doing anything.

I now know that God and my wife both "love a cheerful giver." Truly God wants us to give (money, time and service) but He wants us to do it cheerfully.

See funny video (8 min.) "Scrooge buys his wife a ring".
https://www.truechristianshortstoriesfreebygmmatheny.com/cheerful-giver-or-scrooge-buys-his-wife-a-ring.html

ADVENTURE #3
"He that Winneth Souls"

My first witness.

While in the military, a brother in the navy had invited me to his church. After I had attended for a few weeks, the pastor came up to me at the end of an evening service and asked, "What are you doing tomorrow evening?" I knew there was no service the next night, so I thought he was inviting me over to his house for dinner.

"I'm not doing anything," I replied, expecting a dinner invitation to follow.

But I was surprised to hear, "Good, then I want you to come out tomorrow and go on church visitation."

"Oh, I couldn't do that," I said.

He asked, "Why?"

"I wouldn't know what to say," I said.

"You don't need to say anything. Just be the silent partner," he said and explained to me a silent partner goes to encourage and lets the other person do the talking. I really didn't want to go, but I couldn't think of any way out of it; I had already told him I wasn't busy. So, I agreed to go along.

The next evening, the pastor matched me up with this nineteen-year-old kid, who I found out later really enjoyed arguing. "Let's go get 'em!" he said as we headed for the door. But I didn't want to "get" anyone.

Our first call was at the house of a lady who regularly attended the church, but her son was an atheist. She said, "Oh, good! I'm glad you're here," and sat us down at the kitchen table—her atheist son, my partner, and I, so that we could witness to (argue with) her son. She left the room, leaving me alone with the two of them. They were seated across from each other, while I was on the far end of the table. They talked for about an hour, and each seemed to like making his point. I was waiting for it to be over.

After about forty minutes, the atheist, who was getting a little frustrated, stopped and pointed his finger at me and asked, "What are you doing here?" Up to that time, I had said nothing and had been hoping to get out of there without saying anything. But now he was pointing his finger at me and asking why I had come to his house.

I kind of went blank and stared at him. I thought, "Oh no! Now I've got to say something" and "That's a good question; what am I doing here?" I couldn't think of any real reason why I was there—except, "I just think God wants me to be here."

"Oh," he said, and turned back to my partner and started arguing again. That's all he said to me and that's all I said to him, and guess what? The Holy Spirit gave me joy for that! It was like God was saying to me, *That's good. You finally stood up for me.* It wasn't much—a start, a beginning—but I had this joy. I began to smile, and the atheist looked at me a couple of times trying to figure out what I was so happy about. When we left, I asked my partner, "Where are we going to next?" That was the start of my witnessing for Christ.

Amazing true story

Gia Nguyen and Author Garry Matheny

Gia Thuong Nguyen (That was his name, but we pronounced it "Yar Winn.") had been an officer in the Vietnamese Navy during the Vietnam War. He and his crew patrolled the Mekong Delta in a small, motorized boat to check for Viet Cong, who were using the river. In 1975 Yar Winn was in his boat when news came over the radio that Saigon had fallen to the

North Vietnamese and soldiers, including Yar Winn, were to lay down their arms. They were told they would be put in relocation camps for four months and then returned to their families. But Yar Winn spent the next four years as a POW in a remote jungle prison camp, along with other officers. Each had a small hut separated by a few yards from the others. Apparently, soldiers who were not officers did only spend a relatively short time in confinement and were then released, but not the officers.

Yar Winn said he only had one thing on his mind when he left his confinement: getting out of Vietnam. He couldn't bring himself to live under those whom he had fought. He wanted freedom, and he set his mind on finding a way out of the country. His wife had been raising their two sons in hopes of living together as a family again. He told her of his desire to leave the country on a boat (people who fled during that time period were known as the "Boat People"). She explained to him it meant death if caught, for at that time the new Communist government was cutting the heads off those who were apprehended. She was afraid of risking their lives and the lives of their sons. He told her he would chance it, and if he made it to safety, he would send for her and them. Little did she know the four years she had waited for him while he was a POW would be short in comparison to what lay ahead.

Yar Winn climbed on a boat with some others who were fleeing, and for the better part of a week sailed the high seas. He used his experience as a boat captain and navigated by the stars, and the Lord provided clear nights. They were picked up near Malaysia and taken to a small island and placed in a refugee camp. Getting to the United States took a year while he waited for the paperwork to be processed. Once in America, he found a job and started working on bringing his family to his new home.

Eleven years passed. He tried different ways, including the Red Cross, all eventually leading to a dead end. Part of the problem involved buying plane tickets for his wife and two children: Who would pay? It was in this setting of despair that he received a letter from his wife. It said, in part, what was the point of trying anymore, with years of getting nowhere and prospects growing dim? What hope was there? Remember, he had fought in the war as a naval officer in the South Vietnamese Navy, he had been in a Communist prison camp for four years, had risked his life on the high seas on a log boat, and spent eleven years trying to get his family to him. A man can take a lot, but the loss of one's family seems to some to be insurmountable.

The day he got the letter from his wife, I knocked on his door for the first time. But if it hadn't been for a vow I made to God, I never would have known him. Back when I was in Bible college, I was challenged by a preacher who said Christians should witness to one person a day and try to win one person a week to the Lord. At the invitation, I came forward and made a vow to the Lord in connection with this. Of course, it's the Word of God and His Spirit who save people, but God stills uses individuals to accomplish His will (see Acts 1:8). I was afraid I might not be able to win one person a week, but I knew witnessing to one a day was something I could do. So I made the vow.

This turned out to be easier to say than to do. I figured I would average witnessing to thirty people a month. The first two months I tried, I failed to meet my average. After this I soon "forgot" my vow. After graduation, I went to work as an associate pastor, and at a conference, a preacher challenged me to form a plan on how to reach my goals. I thought about my vow while I listened to the message. I went home and figured the only way to fulfill my vow was to go door-to-door, and I set a day and a time to do this each week. The first month of knocking on doors, I was not successful in reaching my goal, but I did come close; the next month I surpassed my goal. Someone might say, "But that's notching your gun." I suppose a person could look at it that way, but I needed to keep on track to be sure I kept my vow.

I figured I was about 500 behind since I had made the vow. So, time passed with me keeping my vow. I also added extra witnesses at the end of each month to help make up the 500 I was behind on. (I recommend you don't make too many vows, but if you do, God tells us to keep them, see Ecclesiastes 5:4–5). I was able to sustain my vow over the next nine years but still had not made up my backlog, though I had brought it down to about 400. I realized that unless I changed something, I was never going to get it right. I made a new plan: after getting my average of seven witnesses each week, I would not stop—I would continue to tell at least two more people how to be saved. This would subtract an average of 100 a year from what was left.

It was because of this new plan that I met Yar Winn. In fact, it was the first time I had put my new plan into effect that I met him. It was April 24, 1989, on that day I had already spent an hour knocking on doors on both sides of a street and had managed to reach seven witnesses for the week. Then I remembered that I was going to witness to two more as I had planned, so I crossed over to the next street. After talking for a few minutes to a lady at the first house, I went to the house next door, which was Yar Winn's home.

The door was open, but no one was in sight. I knocked on the doorjamb, and from around the corner, a man appeared with a towel wrapped around his head. The towel actually covered his face, so I could not see any of his features. I thought, "This is different." I did not have a clue as to why he had the towel wrapped around his head. I tried to talk to him but I could not understand what he was saying with the towel wrapped around his face. My first instinct was to leave, *but then he fell down right in front of me.* It was then I saw some stains on the towel and asked him if he was bleeding.

He said, "Yes." and that was the first word he uttered that I could understand. He pulled the towel back and exposed his face, which was covered in blood.

When I saw that, a fear gripped me, and I knew something very wrong had happened, but I didn't know what or why. I was not sure if it was an accident, and I was afraid to step inside his house, thinking it might have been domestic violence. So I ran back to the last house I was at and told the lady that her neighbor was bleeding badly and to please call an ambulance. She did, and half of the neighborhood came and filled his living room. Yar Winn's neighbors put him on his couch and tried to help as best they could. He was bleeding from his head, one of his eyes bulged out, and his jaw looked broken.

A bullet had gone in under his chin, with the powder burns visible, and exited at the front of his head just a little inside his hairline. His neighbors asked him what happened and he explained that he had shot himself. The police found out later he had used his 32-caliber pistol.

It was at that moment, with his living room filled with neighbors and Yar Win lying on his couch waiting for the ambulance, bleeding, and with seemingly no chance of survival, that I asked if it would be okay if I had a word of prayer. They all agreed, and we prayed for him. Then I went over to where he was lying and told him I was a preacher. I witnessed to him right then and there. I said, "When the Lord Jesus Christ died, there were two other men that died that day; one was on his right side and the other on his left. Both were thieves, but Jesus only saved one and not the other. The man He saved was not good, not a church member, not baptized, and, being a thief, he hadn't kept the Ten Commandments." (We should do all these good things, but they do not save, forgive our sins, or open the door of Heaven for us.) "The other thief was the same type of sinner, so we can't say one was better than the other. They both believed that Jesus existed. They were both talking to Him." I then asked Yar Winn, "What was the difference? Why did Jesus save the one and not the other?" He looked up at me, but made no response. I answered, "Because one asked Christ to save him; but the other didn't trust Him for it."

I asked, "Could you admit to God that you are a sinner and in need of His forgiveness?" I also asked if he believed that Christ died for his sins and that Christ's body rose from the grave. "Yes," he answered to all these questions. I quoted to him one verse, Romans 10:13: *"For whosoever shall call upon the name of the Lord shall be saved."* I explained to him that "whosoever" meant him, and that the name of the Lord was Jesus (Romans 10:9). Our Savior is not just some "higher power." The Lord Jesus Christ made us and died for us (Colossians 1:13–16), and if we will trust in Him, God said He would save us.

I asked Yar Winn, "Would you like to ask Christ to come into your heart and save you?" Again, he responded yes, and I led him in what we would call a "sinner's prayer." *All* of us are sinners (see Romans 3:23). The difference is that some are forgiven and some are not. It's true you may not have as many sins as some (see Luke 7:47, Genesis 39:9, Isaiah 1:18, John 19:11), but regardless, you and I are sinners, and all sins break fellowship with God and cause us to need

His forgiveness.

The prayer for salvation contains the following:

1. You recognize before God you are a sinner and in need of His forgiveness.
2. You believe Christ died for your sins also.
3. You personally call upon the Lord to forgive you of your sins.
4. You trust Jesus Christ to take you to Heaven when you die.

Yar Winn said he would do all this, but he did it differently than I expected. I had told him to pray in his heart because I could see the bullet had shattered some of his teeth. Instead, he prayed out loud with blood still gurgling in his throat! After he prayed to receive Christ, the police and medics showed up, along with a helicopter. The medical assistant who took his blood pressure said, "I don't know how he is doing it." After shooting himself in the head, he was still conscious and talking! I asked the medics if he would live, and they responded, "We will have to see."

He was flown to Harborview Medical Center in Seattle. The next day, surgeons operated on him to remove the remainder of the bullet, which had not fully exited. I asked the doctor if he thought Yar Winn would live, and if so, what the damage to his brain would be. I was surprised to hear him say, "That area of the brain is not that important." I thought it was all important! He said, "There will be some damage, but to what extent, we can only wait and see." To this day, the only problem I know of is that sometimes Yar Winn experiences blackouts lasting a few minutes (after some years he stopped having the black outs). Other than that, he holds a job and lives a normal life.

He told me later he had never trusted Christ before, but he had watched some religious programs on television. I gave him assurance of his salvation, *"These things have I written unto you that believe on the name of the Son of God; that ye may know that ye have eternal life..."* (I John 5:13). Bible says you can *"know"* that you *"have"* eternal life based upon what is *"written"* in God's Word. All our faith is based on what the Bible says (Romans 10:17), not on our feelings. I'm sure the thief on the cross felt crucified, but he had Christ's promise and so do we: *"For whosoever shall call upon the name of the Lord shall be saved"* (Romans 10:13). If tomorrow you have doubts or you're sick and don't "feel saved," are you going to go by that as your spiritual indicator, or by what God has said? *"If ye will not believe, surely ye shall not be established"* (Isaiah 7:9). In other words, if you don't believe what God has said, how can you know?

Whose opinion or theory are you going to go by? *"But what saith it? The word is nigh thee, even in thy mouth, and in thy heart: that is the word of faith, which we preach; That if thou shalt confess with thy mouth the Lord Jesus, and shalt believe in thine heart that God hath raised him from the dead, thou shalt be saved. For with the heart man believeth unto righteousness; and with the mouth confession is made unto salvation. For the scripture saith, Whosoever believeth on him shall not be ashamed. For there is no difference between the Jew and the Greek: for the same Lord over all is rich unto all that call upon him. For whosoever shall call upon the name of the Lord shall be saved"* (Romans 10:8–13).

Yar Winn came to our church and was baptized and sat in the front row, singing praises to God and memorizing scripture. Our church later raised the money to fly Yar Winn's wife and two sons from Vietnam to the United States. Yar Winn was able to serve as the translator for his wife as one of the sisters in our church led her to the Lord. Their two sons, who received excellent grades in school, went on to graduate from a university. I am happy to say there was another addition to their family, as Yar and his wife later had a third son.

"For what is our hope, or joy, or crown of rejoicing? Are not even ye in the presence of our Lord Jesus Christ at his coming?" (I Thessalonians 2:19)   Part of your joy in Heaven will be from seeing those you have led to Christ!

ADVENTURE #4
How God got my attention!

"Spectacular Wreck" was the title appearing on the front page of the *Everett Herald*, a Washington State newspaper. The headline was followed by: "DRIVER RESCUED - Everett police officers and firemen worked for 40 minutes extracting the driver from this demolished car, which went out of control on the 41st Street Broadway overpass shortly before 3:30 this morning. Assisting in the rescue operation is county coroner Mr. Xon Baker."

When I was eighteen, I almost died in a car wreck. Though I did not turn to God then, the wreck did, indirectly, bring me to Christ. I had been in another accident just one month before, and I had not learned my lesson. This second crash nearly cost me my life. I owned a brand new 1968 Cougar with a 428 Cobra jet engine, and I thought, "I look good behind the wheel of that car!" Of course, the purpose of a fast car is to go *fast*, which I did; too fast for me.

It was early morning, around 3:00, and I'm glad I was alone; otherwise, someone else would have ended up hurt or dead. I was going 125 miles per hour, and at that speed, the valves floated in the engine (thankfully), or I would have been going even faster. I lost control as I approached an overpass. The car spun out and skidded around sideways, leaving eighty feet of skid marks, and hit the corner of the bridge. At impact the tires hit the curb and blew out. Fortunately, my head tilted to one side as the car tipped over, because the bridge tore through the roof and smashed my left shoulder, instead of my head, pushing me into the back seat. Somehow in that moment, there was just enough room for my feet to get out from under the dashboard, but not enough room for my shoes, which stayed under the dash. The force of the crash imbedded the car key, which was in the contact on the dashboard, down to the floor. It crushed the car's body, springing its frame into the shape of a banana.

The roof pinned me into the back seat and I could not breathe! My only thought was, "I don't want to die." With my right hand, I pulled myself up to a position where I could get air into my lungs. It took about thirty minutes for the police to arrive, followed by the fire department. Those who found my car thought no one could have survived, so they also called the mortician. He showed up but, thankfully, wasn't needed. It took another forty-five minutes for the fire department to pry the door open. Where I ended up was literally the only space left in the car. Later, when the insurance adjuster called me, he didn't believe I had remained in the car, but thought I had been thrown out. When I told him I had been trapped inside, he asked, "Where? There's no room!"

I spent a month in the hospital. I broke my left anklebone and still have an aluminum screw in it to this day, a little reminder of my stupidity. I also snapped the tendons in my left shoulder and had some other minor injuries, or so I thought. On the second day at the hospital, I started losing blood in my left kidney. This prompted the doctors to call my parents to come and spend the night with me, as they weren't sure I would make it.

During my first few days at the hospital, I lay unconscious most of the time and only occasionally woke up. It was during one of these few conscious times when something happened to make me change the direction of my life. I woke up and saw my dad looking at me with an expression on his face that seemed to say, "What am I doing raising these kids?" He said nothing; he just had that expression, and I knew he was disappointed in me. At that moment it was hard for him. I was going around doing my own thing, not concerned with or even considering others' feelings, but I didn't like seeing my dad look like that. I felt like I had let him down, and I didn't want to disappoint him. I made a decision then to do something that would please him, and not me. Without realizing it, I began to obey the Bible— *"Honor thy father."* No, this did not save me nor forgive my sins, but there is a promise attached to this commandment found in Deuteronomy

5:16, *"that it may go well with thee."* My dad and mom loved me and were good to me, and I wanted to do something that would make them happy.

A few months after the doctors released me from the hospital, Dad took me to the navy recruiter. It was something I never would have done on my own. I guess Dad was concerned about my circle of friends and the direction I was going in, which was *nowhere!* So, I signed up! Later, something happened in the military I had never experienced before.

About six times, people came up to me and started talking about God, or at least they tried to. I refused to talk to the first person who tried this, but eventually I started to listen. They talked about being "saved."

"What do you mean, 'saved'?" I asked

"Will you go to Heaven when you die?" they responded.

"I'll find out when I die!" I said.

"That's too late. What if you wake up in Hell?" they replied.

About the only time I remember talking about the Lord before this was when I used His name in vain. The church I was brought up in never said *only* Jesus Christ could save you, or even talked about how to be saved. The Holy Spirit started working on me, and I thought maybe there was something to all of this. And if God made me, then He should know how I could find happiness. The car wreck had made me realize I was not "Mr. Indestructible." I began to think about death and eternity. This life compared to eternity is only a split second. So, after death where was I going?

ADVENTURE #5
Parachuting

Your first birth is not good enough to get you to Heaven! We were born sinners, not Christians (Psalm 51:5). That's why the Bible says, *"You must be born again."* There is much confusion on this. Nonetheless, the Bible says you *"must"* be born again (John 3:7). It is a *spiritual* birth. *"That which is born of the flesh is flesh;* [your first birth] *and that which is born of the Spirit is spirit"* (John 3:6). Only God can give this. It is *"not of yourself,"* it is not the gift of the church or the gift of the minister, but the *"gift of God"* (Ephesians 2:8). We could no more give ourselves this spiritual birth than we could give ourselves a physical birth. We could not merit, work for, earn, or buy our physical birth. The same with our spiritual birth. Someone else has to give it to us. Just as our mothers gave us the physical birth, so the Spirit of God must give us the spiritual birth. There is a major difference, however. We had *no say* in the physical birth, but we do in the spiritual birth. *"For whosoever shall call upon the name of the Lord shall be saved"*

(Romans 10:13).

The Bible says, *"Not of works, lest any man should boast"* (Ephesians 2:9). Can you imagine long lines of sinners at the judgment, with each person bragging to God about how good he or she has been? Would you want to listen to that? How much less God! *"Therefore we conclude that a man is justified by faith without the deeds of the law"* (Romans 3:28). Even if it were possible, and it is not, to live a perfect life without sin from this moment forward, what would you do with all the sins you have committed thus far? *"For the wages of sin is death"* (Romans 6:23). Not good deeds or a slap on the wrist, but death. *"But God commendeth his love toward us, in that, while we were yet sinners, Christ died for us."* (Romans 5:8)

You may be thinking, "This is too easy." I used to agree with you. I thought, "God will forgive all my sins and take me to Heaven, just for trusting Him to do this?" Somehow, while I was growing up, I had been given the impression I could earn my salvation. But the Bible taught something else. About the time I was contemplating this, an unexpected event gave me a clear focus on why I could not save myself.

While in the navy, some friends and I one evening talked about parachuting out of an airplane. This was not for the military, but on our free time. The next day when we met at the airport, only one of my friends showed up; the rest chickened out! There were eight civilians at the hangar, plus my buddy and I. We all listened to four hours of instructions on "How to jump out of an airplane with a parachute."

I'm a little afraid of heights, and I remember thinking, "Am I really going to do this?" The instructor said it was like jumping off a table onto sand. It's actually more like jumping off a roof onto cement. Everyone was listening very intently to the instructor, but I was wishing I was someplace else, and trying to think of a way to get out of it.

When the time came for us to get into the plane, they *all ran* to the aircraft—except me. I just stood there watching them and thinking how brave they all were. So, I walked to the plane, telling myself, "If they can do this, so can I." I was too dumb to know that the last person in the plane would be the first person to jump out!

I sat right next to the door, as there was no other space left. In fact, there was no door at all, just an opening where the door normally would have been, but it had been removed for parachuting. You'd think I should have known, sitting there next to the door, that I would be the first one out of the plane, but it still had not dawned on me. And I still wasn't sure I wanted to jump, but I was positive I did not want to be the first one out and demonstrate to everyone else how to do it.

The plane took off, and I watched everything on the ground get farther away. I was thinking to myself, "How did I get in this position?" Then I noticed the rip cords from our parachutes had been placed on a metal bar as we got into the plane, so when we jumped out, we did not pull our own rip cord; it automatically opened as we left the plane. I studied that for a minute, and I noticed that my rip cord was on top of everyone else's. A horrifying thought came over me. I turned and said to the instructor, "Hey, I'm not the first one out, am I?" Everyone looked at me and nodded their heads; some even laughed out loud.

When the airplane reached the elevation of three thousand feet, the pilot cut the engine and the instructor told me, "Get out on the wing." I had served in the military for three years by this time, and when someone gave me an order, I just obeyed. So out on the wing I went! At an altitude of three thousand feet, the trees only look about a quarter-inch tall, and as I peered down, fear gripped my whole body. I thought, "Idiot, what are you doing here?" The instructor hollered at me to jump. I looked at him and nodded my head in the affirmative, but when I again glanced down, I couldn't let go. This was repeated several times, with the instructor yelling at me to jump and with me nodding my head yes, but not able to let go of the plane. There I stood, stuck on this plane's wing. I saw the instructor talking to the pilot. They were not sure what to do with me. Later, I found out they were considering landing the plane *with me on the wing!*

Everyone was watching me with their faces pushed up against the window, wondering if I was really going to jump or not. All I could think was, "How did I get myself in this position?" And more importantly, "How was I going to get out of it? How does everyone else get out of this?" I thought, "I know: they use their parachute. Yes, this is really stupid, and I will never do it again, but this parachute will work at least one more time." So, I let go of the plane!

***

I told this story at church once, and after the service, an elderly lady came up to me and asked,

"Sonny, did it work?"

"Did what work?" I asked.

"You know, the parachute, did it work?"

"Well, yes, Ma'am, I am here."

***

Why the above story? Because like millions of others, I thought, "I believe there is a God, and if I'm really good, I can go to Heaven." That's like saying, "I believe in this parachute, but I'm not letting go of the plane." If I had told the instructor, "I'm trusting the parachute," then he would have hollered, "Let go of the plane!" In your daily walk, please be good, but good works will never pay for bad things (sins). This can only be done by trusting Christ. To trust the parachute, I had to let go of the plane. And to trust Christ, I had to let go of my baptism, my few good deeds, and my religion. I had to put my faith only in Christ.

You might think this sounds too easy; but it is not as simple as it sounds. For twenty-three years I had believed in *my* way to get to Heaven;

but to trust God's Son, I had to stop trusting all I had depended on before and trust someone I had never seen, taking Him only at His Word. When people say, "Hey, I'm trusting Christ and, if I'm really good, I will go to Heaven," they're not trusting Christ, but being "good" to get to Heaven! Let go of the plane!

Are you lost?
"For the Son of man is come to seek and to save that which was lost."
(Luke 19:10)

"For this my son was dead, and is alive again; he was lost, and is found. And they began to be merry." (Luke 15:24)

When I asked Christ to save me, I did not say "Come into my heart" or "Forgive all my sins," though I meant all of that and more. All I actually said with my voice when I received Jesus as my Savior was, "Yes, Lord, I believe in you." I now trust Jesus Christ to get me to Heaven; and if He does not get me there, I will never go, because my faith is not in anyone or anything else! But I believe it is as God has said: *"Believe on the Lord Jesus Christ and thou shalt be saved"* (Acts 16:31). Man's way gives the glory to man, by bragging on ourselves about how good we are, but in God's way, *only* Jesus will receive the glory because our faith is in Him, not in ourselves and what we have done.

"But what saith it? The word is nigh thee, even in thy mouth, and in thy heart: that is, the word of faith, which we preach; That if thou shalt confess with thy mouth the Lord Jesus, and shalt believe in thine heart that God hath raised him from the dead, thou shalt be saved. For with the heart man believeth unto righteousness; and with the mouth confession is made unto salvation." (Romans 10:8–10).

A gift, though it be free, is still not yours till you receive it. By simple faith, ask Jesus Christ to save you. I am not talking about saying prayers for daily needs, concerns, or problems, which we should also pray for, but more importantly, ask Christ to save you so you can go to Heaven. Some have put faith in their prayer, not in Jesus, to save them. Even if they ask Christ a thousand times to save them, until they trust Him to do this, they are not saved! No one else can do this for you.

You can receive Christ right now! The

following is a model prayer that one can say to God: "Dear God, I believe that Jesus Christ is Your only begotten Son. I believe He died in my place for my sins, and that He rose again from the grave. And right now, I ask Him to save me. Dear Lord Jesus, please forgive me of my sins and come into my heart, and when I die take my soul to Heaven. For I pray this in your name, Lord Jesus." Could you pray from your heart such a prayer? God promises to save all who will do this, *"For whosoever shall call upon the name of the Lord shall be saved"* (Romans 10:13).

ADVENTURE #6
A Fish Story, But True!

The closest some will ever get to revival is when they get a hold of this thing called "giving." Remember the story of Ebenezer Scrooge? (A Christmas Carol by Charles Dickens) He was a cold-hearted miser until he learned the joy of giving.

We can learn a lesson from the Dead Sea, it has no outlet because it's the lowest spot on earth. It's called the "Dead" Sea for good reason. Nothing lives in it—too many pollutants and too much salt. If the Dead Sea had an outlet, it would cleanse itself and be like the Sea of Galilee, with fish in it. Both the Sea of Galilee and the Dead Sea are fed by the Jordan River, but only one has an outlet. The other retains everything it receives and only loses water through evaporation. Are you a "Dead Sea" Christian with no outlet—one who only receives and does not give?

It has been said that there are two types of people— "givers" and "takers." Which are you? I can guarantee that the givers are happier. *"I have shewed you all things, how that so labouring ye ought to support the weak, and to remember the words of the Lord Jesus, how he said, It is more blessed to give than to receive"* (Acts 20:35). What was your happiest Christmas? We all like receiving gifts, but can you recall a gift you gave that put a smile on someone's face, and one in your heart?

Abraham and Jacob tithed hundreds of years before the law. Jesus said, *"Woe unto you, scribes and Pharisees, hypocrites! for ye pay tithe of mint and anise and cummin, and have omitted the weightier matters of the law, judgment, mercy, and faith: these ought ye to have done, and not to leave the other undone."* The *"other"* in this context was the tithe. There are other things that are much more important than tithing, as *"the law, judgment, mercy, and faith"*, and we should concentrate on these, but not forget to tithe. If you cannot trust God with your money, how can you trust Him at all? God will take care of you! *"Give, and it shall be given unto you..."* (Luke 6:38).

There is only one place in the Bible where God says, *"Prove me,"* and it is with tithes and offerings. *"Bring ye all the tithes into the storehouse, that there may be meat in mine house, and prove me now herewith, saith the LORD of hosts, if I will not open you the windows of Heaven, and pour you out a blessing, that there shall not be room enough to receive it"* (Malachi 3:10). When God says *"prove me,"* He is saying, *"Find out if I am real. Find out if I can keep my promises; prove me!"* Why does God do it with money? Because we all know how much money we have left at the end of the month, and when we see that God blesses us, yes, even financially, then we say to ourselves, "God can keep all the other promises in the Bible, too." God is not afraid of your taking Him at His Word. Are you afraid? Let God get a hold of your heart in this area and have joy, one of the fruits of the Holy Spirit!

"There shall not be room to receive it" (Malachi 3:10)

His name was Merle, and he was a commercial fisherman and a member of our church. He was faithful to the church and a good brother, who enjoyed tithing. We had held a stewardship conference in our church and one of our main goals was to raise money for a new church building. That night after the conference,

Merle said to his wife, "Let's pray about what our commitment should be this year."

"Okay," she said, and then added, "But let's pray separately. I'll go upstairs and pray, and you pray downstairs. I don't want to hear you praying out loud about some amount we should give, and that number being placed in my head." He agreed, and in a few minutes she came downstairs and asked, "How much do you think God wants us to give?"

Now, the number God had put on Merle's heart was $3,000, but he was afraid to tell his wife the amount, so he asked her, "What do *you* think we should give?"

"I asked you first," she responded.

"Well, I think we should give three thousand" he said.

His wife smiled and said, "Yes, that's what I also believe God spoke to my heart about." He was happy when he heard her say that.

As a commercial fisherman in Washington State, Merle fished for salmon in Puget Sound. As his money came in, he would go to the bank and put it in his account, in what he called "winter money." He explained to me with his overhead and all, he needed $12,000 to get through the winter. He might make it with $10,000, but he really should have $12,000. Every time he deposited the winter money into his account, he felt convicted. "God first" is what the Bible says (Matthew 6:33). Merle said, "I prayed every time I deposited money: 'Lord I did not forget about you. I just need my winter money first.'"

Have you ever done anything like this? Some people save their tithe until they see a need at church and then give, but it is not theirs; it is the Lord's (Leviticus 27:30). Waiting or procrastinating not only makes a temptation to spend what is rightly the Lord's, but also brings guilt. When we make the decision to establish regular giving (Malachi 3:8–10, I Corinthians 16:1–2), it keeps us from fighting with it, and we can then have joy. Hey, if we are going to do it, let's do it right! Merle said no matter what he said to the Lord, the conviction remained, so he got his checkbook and wrote a check for $3,000 for the building fund. Mind you, this was over and above his regular tithe.

We were at the church when Merle walked up to me and gave me the $3,000 check. He explained it was for the building fund and told me the story I just shared with you. He reminded me about his winter money and said, "Pastor, I only had $5,000 in the bank and now after this check to the church, I will only have $2,000." I know there are some who would have given the money back, feeling sorry for him, but if someone has more faith than you, don't stand in the way of their faith. He was following a biblical principle: Jesus first! Did Jesus give the widow's two mites back after she put them in the collection plate? Twice Christ said she gave all, *"all that she had, even all her living"* *(Mark 12:41-44). And the state had no welfare programs in her day, so what would she eat? You can be assured God took care of her (see I Kings 17:11-15).

When Merle gave me the check, he reminded me there was only a month left for fishing and it had not been a good season. That night, as God would have it, he got a phone call that the fish were running and he could go fishing. Washington State regulates this; you cannot just go salmon fishing when and where you please. He fished with a 32-foot "bow-picker," as he called it, which meant the boat had a large metal drum on the front that would bring the net in. This type of fishing is called "gill netting," a net with square holes lets smaller fish swim through but catches the bigger salmon.

Those fishing on the sound that night were to fish between a buoy and a designated point on the shore, a sort of invisible line in the water. If you went past this invisible line, the coast guard would remind you where it was by giving you a fine! The best place to catch fish was to get as close as possible to this invisible line without going over it. Almost all the salmon ran in one direction between the shore and this buoy. The problem was, with all the boats in Merle's group, there just wasn't room for everyone on this line. The first boats out would get the best location right up to the line. Those who showed up later would have to stay behind the front row of boats, which meant they could only catch whatever fish swam around the front nets. In fact, it was even worse if a boat got stuck in the center with other boats all around it, because then it was difficult to catch the salmon that sometimes ran from the other direction.

Well, Merle got stuck in the center! I can remember him telling me, "Pastor, it was the worst place to be." He said he was upset. "Pastor,

I tried everything I could to get there early, but there were problems with the boat, and we got stuck in the middle!" He told me he would have gone back to shore, but doing that would have run over others' nets. His deckhand talked him into letting down his net, and he told him maybe they would at least catch enough fish to pay for the fuel. They put out their net and hooked it up to the metal drum. That's when it happened— God's blessing!

Merle said the drum that was bringing in the net started making noise and slipping. He thought he had snagged a log. Then he saw the fish flashing in the water, and I can remember him telling me, "Pastor, in that first set I counted almost 150 salmon, the next set about seventy, the third set about a hundred." Then he added, "On the front line, two boats did really good. One caught close to 450 fish and another peaked at 500. That's big-time fishing out on Puget Sound!" He paused and then said, "Pastor, do you know how many fish I caught last night? I caught one thousand, one hundred salmon!" He told me later he had been fishing for over twenty years out on Puget Sound and had never caught that many fish.

Merle then quoted a portion of Malachi 3:10, saying, "There was not *'room enough to receive'* them all." He explained that as he was bringing in the last set, his boat was so heavy with fish, its bow started to dip into the water. His deckhand said that they would sink if he insisted on trying to get the last set in. Merle told me that when you finish fishing, you were to bring the salmon in by the shore and unload them into a barge. But he was already full, and he didn't know what to do with the fish still in the net in the water. He couldn't get them in the boat, and there was no way he could drag that long net all the way to the barge without getting it tangled up or other boats running over it. He said, "You just can't leave a set of fish setting there in the water. I didn't know what to do, and don't get me wrong, Pastor, I'm not greedy, but God gave me those fish and I wanted them!"

He told me the other fishing boats saw what was happening, and after they had unloaded their fish, they untied the barge and brought it out to him so he could unload his boat and bring in his last set. He said he had never seen this done before, bringing the barge out to a boat. And this because there wasn't *"room enough to receive"* them all.

When he was telling me this, I remember thinking, "I wish I could be a fisherman." God couldn't do that for a pastor or a plumber or a fry cook, could he? God says, *"Prove me."* When people find out that God is able to keep His Word in connection with giving, they begin to believe and obey other commands in the Bible!

"And Simon answering said unto him, Master, we have toiled all the night, and have taken nothing: nevertheless at thy word I will let down the net. And when they had this done, they enclosed a great multitude of fishes: and their net brake. And they beckoned unto their partners, which were in the other ship, that they should come and help them. And they came, and filled both the ships, so that they began to sink. When Simon Peter saw it, he fell down at Jesus' knees, saying, Depart from me; for I am a sinful man, O Lord. For he was astonished, and all that were with him, at the draught of the fishes which they had taken: And so was also James, and John, the sons of Zebedee, which were partners with Simon. And Jesus said unto Simon, Fear not; from henceforth thou shalt catch men" (Luke 5:5–10). *"Now unto him that is able to do*

exceeding abundantly above all that we ask or think, according to the power that worketh in us" (Ephesians 3:20).

ADVENTURE #7
Special Operation
of a Nuclear Submarine
TRUE STORY

    I was a diver in the navy from 1971-1975, and all us divers on our submarine had received top secret clearances. I was not a SEAL but a saturation diver, trained for deep dives and extended periods of time. I made five saturation dives in the navy and three of them lasted one week each - explained later.

About eight years ago, I corresponded a few times with John Piña Craven. He was an officer in the US Navy and, in fact, was the Chief Scientist of the Special Projects Office of the United States Navy. He has a bachelor's degree from Cornell University, a master's of science degree from California Institute of Technology, a PhD from University of Iowa, and a law degree from George Washington University.

Craven published the book *The Silent War: The Cold War Battle Beneath the Sea*. He guided the navy's undersea special-projects operations during the Cold War, and we owe him a debt of gratitude for his service.

In his book, he talks about the project I was involved in, and he writes about it in the first person (not hearsay). How he was able to do this without crossing over the legal line, I cannot tell, but aside from being a scientist, he was also a lawyer. I will quote him on the secret parts.

The nuclear submarine USS *Halibut*, while it was still in service, had the distinction of being the most highly decorated submarine of the post-WWII era. What follows is somewhat technical, but there is a point to it all. I joined the navy as a reservist and originally had a two-year active-duty obligation, but I kept extending my time so I could attend three navy diving schools. In all, I served nearly five years on active duty and more than a year reserve time. The navy sent me to two diving schools in Washington, D.C.: second-class dive school, a ten-week diving and salvage school; and first-class dive school, which lasted seventeen-weeks. I graduated top in my class from both. In addition, I graduated fourth in my class from the navy's saturation dive school at Point Loma, California, which was about a fourteen-week program.

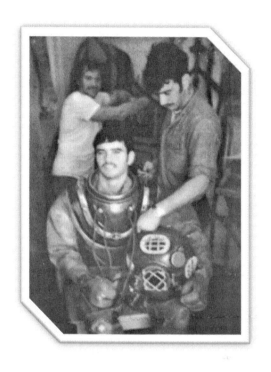

In 1975, there were 200 saturation divers in the navy, and basically, we either went to experimental diving stations or to special operations. I ended up in special ops on the fast-attack nuclear-powered submarine USS *Halibut* SSN-587, a 350-foot vessel with two levels in the middle section and a crew of 130 men, plus more than twenty divers.

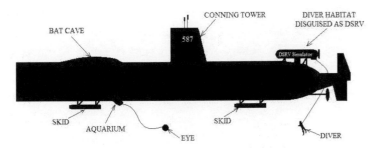

No other submarine had the unique silhouette of the USS *Halibut* (see picture and also drawing above). There was a huge metal bubble on the deck of our sub, named the "bat cave"; it was situated halfway between the bow of the sub and the conning tower. Then, on the tail end was something that looked like the Deep Submergence Rescue Vessel (DSRV). Once, when we were on the surface and coming into San Francisco Bay under the Golden Gate Bridge, a newscaster who was in a helicopter reported seeing our sub, and he described it as looking like it was pregnant (bat cave) and carrying a baby on its back (DSRV).

I loved the stealth, secrecy, and capabilities of submarines, from the red lights that glowed at night in the main control room (so that if we surfaced, we could see immediately without needing to adjust our eyes to the darkness), to the eighteen-hour days (we slept six hours, worked six hours, and studied six hours. Because it was all done underwater, one never knew if it was night or day except by looking at his watch.).

The following are a few of John Piña Craven's quotes when speaking of our submarine: "The *Halibut* was responsible for the success of at least two of the most significant espionage missions of our time" (*The Silent War*, p. 140). There were many major technical difficulties for the overhaul of the *Halibut* to make it ready for these operations, however, he said, "But I think these problems pale beside the importance and ultimate impact of the intelligence operations that *Halibut* would be involved in and the grave dangers she would face" (p. 142), more on this further on.

At this time in the life of our sub, it had become a diving platform and existed to take us divers where we needed to go. We would make our dives and then return to port; our missions (unless training) would last from two to three months. In all, I was attached to the USS *Halibut* for a year and a half.

During this time, I was asked by an officer, who oversaw security for our mission, what I thought about the special operation. My response was then, and still is today, "Our enemies do similar things to us, and we would be irresponsible not to do the same." While we were in port, the navy would send out teams to try to find out what we were doing, with the idea that if they could discover our mission, then our security was not good enough. A cover story was created to disguise the actual mission, and we were told to stay out of certain stores because of the possible connection with what we were doing.

In preparation for our special ops, we would make training dives in excess of 400 feet in depth, which lasted seven days. We stayed in a diving chamber during this period and were in the water for a few hours each day. To breathe air at such a depth would make one dangerously drunk (called *nitrogen narcosis*), so we breathed a special mix of helium and oxygen. The seven days were divided into three days at depth and four days of decompression.

Decompression is when the built-up helium in the bloodstream is given time to come out, so bubbles will not form in the diver's blood. At 400 feet, the pressure on your body would be twelve times greater than on the surface. The inside of a submarine is kept at one atmosphere (what we have on the surface), so if a door is opened to the sea, such as a door on the bottom of a submarine, the seawater would immediately enter and flood the sub. But our diving chamber was kept at the same pressure as the outside water, in our case twelve times greater than on the surface (or twelve atmospheres), so when we opened a door on the bottom of our diving chamber, the water would not come in. But this extra pressure means divers would be breathing twelve times as much gas in one breath as they would on the surface. All this "extra" gas would be forced into a diver's lungs and then into his bloodstream, which is why we decompressed—to give time for the gas to come out of our bloodstream.

It is called *saturation diving* because in a dive of more than twelve hours, the bloodstream becomes saturated with whatever gases (in our case, helium and oxygen) a diver breathes, and he cannot take any more into his bloodstream unless he goes deeper.

Saturation Diving Control Room
Alamy /Military Collection

Once our boat (and it is proper to call a submarine either a boat or sub) arrived at our dive station, it was positioned in close proximity to where the dives needed to be made. Our sub had side thrusters on it and could actually go sideways at a couple of knots per hour.

These dives were manned from two control rooms. The small control room or "secondary control room", run by the divers, looked like the inside of a space capsule, and I loved it! It seated two people and contained more than sixty valves, plus pressure gauges for the different gasses and depth gauges for the pressure inside the different compartments within the diving chamber. This cramped control room housed about two dozen small lights on the display console, which blinked if something went wrong. In addition, two TV monitors were squeezed into the space, as the navy monitored most everything we did on camera, both inside the diving chamber and outside in the water. We also used a round, self-propelled, two-foot-diameter TV camera with little thrusters that turned and moved about in the water, which we called the "swimming eyeball" or "eye". This was controlled from the main control room, which was in the area of our sub's periscopes, where the diving officer and master diver sat.

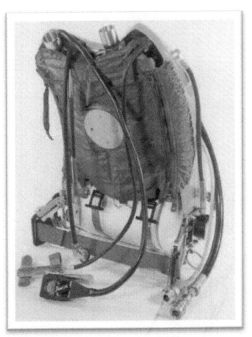

The diving rigs were Westinghouse "Abalone" or Mk 11. After development and testing, the rumored price was 3 million for 6 rigs!

The actual diving chamber, from which the dives were made, was situated directly next to the secondary control room and had space for four divers. We slept, ate, took sponge baths, and made our dives from this small, three-room, tube-shaped diving chamber, which we were not able to completely stand up in because the ceiling was too low. One room was for "pressing down" more divers or a medical officer in the event of an emergency, a second was for sleeping and housed a toilet and sink, and the third was the lockout chamber, where divers prepared to enter the water. Each room or compartment of the chamber was separated by round metal doors more than an inch-thick, which could withstand the extreme pressures at that depth. In addition, there was also a small, two-foot-by-one-foot chamber to convey food back and forth to the divers.

Owing to the necessity of breathing helium and oxygen in place of nitrogen and oxygen (air), we used a special communication system that unscrambled our speech so we would not sound like Donald Duck, an effect brought on by the helium on our vocal cords. Attached to each diver were five hoses or cables 350 feet long: the hot-water cable, a wire cable to pull us back in the event of an emergency, a communication cable, and one hose that pushed our gas to us, and one that pulled it back so no bubbles would reach the surface and no one would know we were there.

One may be thinking that, because of the cables connected to me I was not able to swim around freely, like scuba diving. That's true, but I didn't want to. The depths were too deep for scuba diving. At that depth, when a diver has his bloodstream saturated with the gas he is breathing, if he swam only halfway to the surface, he would die.

The sea held little scenery at 400 feet, only some giant king crabs and strange-looking fish about eighteen inches long, with heads almost half the size of their bodies and eyeballs bigger than a human's. They were not afraid of us divers and swam right up to us and stared. They even sat in the silt at the sea bottom, still gazing at us, which seemed eerie.

We dove between "windows" in the tides to prevent fighting the currents and for better visibility, which in the frigid blackness was only about six feet. The sea's temperature was 27 degrees Fahrenheit and would have been frozen solid had it not been saltwater. Because of this us divers wore two wet suits, one eighth-inch-thin rubber suit and one three-eighths-inch thick, with hot water pumped between the two to prevent hypothermia. We needed the eighth-inch liner so the 140-degree water would not scald us. Before a dive, I put my hand into the seawater just to see how cold it felt, and I could not hold my hand in it. The saltwater tried to freeze the blood in my hand, and I could feel it go up my arm and into my heart!

On one dive, some gas leaked under my face mask, which was attached to the liner. The gas seeped over my head and got trapped under the liner, causing my face mask to rise up on my face. On my second dive, I didn't want to fight with my face mask again, so I had this "bright" idea to cut two small holes in the thin liner, so any bubbles could go through it and not cause my mask to rise up. The problem was, I didn't realize it would take time for the hot water to circulate up that high in my wet suit, so when I entered the sea, in came the *freezing cold water* straight to my head. It felt like someone was driving two spikes into my brain! I wasn't sure what to do, and when those in control kept asking through our communication system why I was not moving out, I stalled for time. A diver just didn't bail out and crawl back in the dive chamber; he might not be allowed to make the dive and another diver could take his place.

Fortunately, after a few minutes and a terrible headache, the hot water circulated up to my head, and I was able to perform the dive.

Our Westinghouse diving rigs were semi-rebreathers. We rebreathed our mixed gas, only one in six breaths was a fresh supply of oxygen and helium. Our dive rig would scrub the carbon dioxide that we exhaled, and the fresh gas mix was supplied by our hoses. Our semi-rebreather also heated the mixed gas we breathed, as the freezing water made the mixed gas so cold, it would give you a headache. Our face mask was doubled sealed, one seal around our face and one around our mouth and nose, so if our face mask flooded, we could still breathe. There was also a head set and speaker inside our mask for communications and a red light that came on in the event our gas mix was somehow blocked. This red light was triggered by the use of an emergency tank with a ten-minute supply of gas so we could get back to our dive chamber.

We wanted to make the dives.

I gave this technical part just to get to this point. There were twenty-one saturation divers on the sub, but only eight divers would make the two saturation dives necessary for this operation. The others would man the two control-rooms, which would run nonstop during the dives. More than eight of us wanted to make these dives, and those in charge would not tell us who would dive until we were two weeks out to sea. We had practiced a year for this one special operation, and I definitely wanted to be one of the eight chosen. My desire to make the dive had become so strong and important to me that I began to base all my decisions around it.

The reason this operation was so important

to me was because it was important! All the divers knew that those who would make the dive would be put in for one of the highest medals our nation gives: The Legion of Merit.

The Legion of Merit

We were bound by secrecy, and most of the submariners on our sub did not even know where our sub had gone, let alone what we were doing. But the Legion of Merit would be a witness that we had participated in something of great value to America. In short, it would make me feel like I had done something more than practice. I accept that, for some people, a medal was not necessary or important, but it was to me.

The operation, which continued after I left the navy in 1975, remained safe until the 1980s, when it was compromised by National Security Agency (NSA) cryptologist Ronald W. Pelton. Pelton was tried and convicted of espionage and sentenced to three concurrent life sentences at the federal correction institution, of Allenwood, Pennsylvania.

In his book *The Silent War*, John Craven said, "The KGB succeeded in recruiting … [Ronald W. Pelton, who] … would betray how the *Navy had tapped Soviet underwater communications cables, including the crucial role of saturation diving in those operations*" (p. 278–279).

God Was Working

While on the submarine, I wrestled with whether or not I would serve God. There was a Bible study on the sub that I had been to a few times, and to be honest, I was a little concerned about others seeing me go to it. I thought if I attended the meetings, others would poke fun at me, and more importantly (though I now know unfounded), I had this thought I might not be chosen for the dive. There were at least three officers who would take part in the decision process, and any one of them could stop a diver from making the dive. I can see now I was too concerned about what other people thought.

Happily, God had His faithful witnesses on our sub, who were more concerned about the Lord. I had trusted Christ a few months prior to being assigned to the sub, and on the *Halibut* I met I a man who I will call "Chief". He explained a lot about God and His Word, and I always had questions for him. One day, while I was asking him a question, he said,

"Garry, you ought to go to Bible college."

"Yeah, right, Chief," I replied, laughing.

I had no intention of going to any college, let alone Bible college, but after he said that, I never quite got the idea out of my head. And God used him greatly to encourage me in my Christian life. God had also placed another Christian brother on this submarine, who I will call "Preacher." He led a Bible study, and on Sunday he preached. I had never heard preaching before in my life. It wasn't some sermonizing from a denominational textbook, but standing up and declaring God's Word, and it stirred my heart.

Though teaching the Bible is also of our Lord, God chooses preaching as one of His main ways to grab hold of people (I Corinthians 1:21). Teaching is giving out information but preaching has urgency in it. The purpose of preaching is to bring change, not to fill you with information.

As I said before, I was afraid I might not make the dive if I was seen going with the "God squad" (as the Christians were called) to the Bible studies. One time when on my way to a Bible study, a couple of submariners stopped me and wanted to talk. But I was in a hurry and was trying to figure out some way to leave without them asking where I was going. But they kept on talking without giving me a chance to speak. I finally caught on that they were doing it intentionally because they had figured out where I was going. This was before all the electronic games and there is not much recreation on a submarine, and finding someone to poke fun at becomes a favorite pastime.

"I've got to go," I finally said.

"Well don't be late for your prayer time." They got a laugh out of it.

"Yeah, and I will pray for you!" I responded. And I pulled out my Bible that I had hid in my pocket and went to the Bible study.

Struggling with a decision.

To me, making this dive was a dream come true. I remember praying, "Lord, please let me make this dive." I told the Lord I would start going to the Bible study regularly after the dive and live a better life for Him. But I kept getting this feeling the Lord only wanted to know one thing: *"What if I don't let you make this dive?"* I told the Lord, "I really want to make this dive. It's very important to me." And again, I had the same impression, but only stronger, that the Lord was saying to me, *"What if I don't let you?"*

"Lord," I pleaded, "please let me. It's really important to me." But I could not shake the thought out of my head, *"If I don't let you, will you still serve me anyway?"* It seemed like a bitter cup to drink. I felt heartsick, thinking about being passed over and someone else taking my place. And the only thing I thought the Lord wanted to know was, *"What if I don't let you?"* There is only one response the Lord wants in a situation like this: do what He wants, even if you don't get what you want. I said, "Okay, Lord, I will serve you even if you don't let me make the dive," and then I added, "but I really would like to do this." The Lord likes it when you put the decision in His hands, where it needs to be.

The next day, the diving officer walked up to me and said, "You're making the first dive," and then he walked off. I was thankful to the Lord, and I thought that since I had planned to go to the Bible study after the dive, why not start before it, which I did.

The Dives

As I said before, these particular dives lasted seven days, but we were actually only in the water three times on the first saturation dive. Each wet dive (actually in the water) was carried out with two divers in the water, about two hours at a time. I accomplished the first water entry and served as lead diver on the third one.

After the submarine returned to port, I fulfilled my last month of active duty and was discharged from the navy, and then I registered for Bible college.

The Navy awarded me the Legion of Merit for this dive, along with all the divers who got in the water. The commendation I received reads as follows: "SW2 [DV] Garry M. Matheny, USN. Deployed for a second and even more arduous deployment. During this 96-day deployment he participated in a submarine operation of great importance to the government of the United States. Although description of this operation is precluded by security constraints, the ratee performed in a hostile environment under great operational stress requiring exceptional courage, constant vigilance and keen professional competence. His performance in that environment was superb and was a key factor in the ship's success in that operation."

It was signed by C. R. Larson, Capt. USN Commanding Officer. (Captain Charles R. Larson later became a four-star admiral and was given command of the entire Pacific. Born November 20, 1936—Died July 26, 2014.)

Farewell to a great submarine, the USS *Halibut*.
She was decommissioned at Mare Island California in June of 1976.

(Since writing this our operation has been declassified and **I published** GOD & SPIES: BASED ON A TRUE STORY, TOP SECRET

OPERATION by G.M. Matheny. Both Kindle and paperback, 300 pages. See end of this book.)

ADVENTURE #8
Heavenly Rewards

There are many verses in the Bible about earning rewards. Salvation is a free gift (Romans 5:15–16, Ephesians 2:8–9), but you can earn rewards after you are saved, and it is also possible to lose rewards (see I Corinthians 3:11–15, Colossians 2:18, II Timothy 2:5, II John 1:8, and Revelation 3:11). Rewards are based on many different things. *"And whosoever shall give to drink unto one of these little ones a cup of cold water only in the name of a disciple, verily I say unto you, he shall in no wise lose his reward"* (Matthew 10:42). The Bible tells us God will pass out five different types of crowns when we arrive in Heaven, plus other types of rewards. The best part is that rewards are given by an impartial Judge who makes no mistakes.

Some believe crowns to be symbolic and not literal, but in the book of Revelation, the twenty-four elders in Heaven have literal crowns that they lay down at our Savior's feet. It is possible to earn more than one crown, and when Christ returns, He has *"many crowns."* History tells us a story about two Egyptian kings, one from the north and one from the south, who battled each other. The one who conquered the other took both crowns, combined them, and fashioned one new crown. Perhaps something similar will happen if you earn more than one crown: Christ will create a single crown with parts from the different ones.

As any parent knows, if you give out candy to your children, you must make sure there is enough to go around, or someone will cry or there will be a fight. We may pretend that rewards and crowns are not important to us, but I have not yet been able to talk anyone into giving me their rewards when we get to Heaven. The point is, you will want whatever Jesus Christ is passing out, including rewards. There will be some who receive rewards, and some without rewards, and there will be some given praise, and some without praise (Luke 19:16–22). I do not believe we will be punished in Heaven, for all our punishment was received by Christ on the cross. But there will be shame when Christ returns for His own. *"And now, little children, abide in him; that, when he shall appear, we may have confidence, and not be ashamed before him at his coming."* (I John 2:28). The term "little children" was used by the Apostle John for believers and he said some would have confidence, and some would be ashamed.

And it appears one way we will worship Him throughout all eternity is to lay at His feet rewards that He helped us earn, as the twenty-four elders do in Revelation 4:10.

"Must I go, and empty-handed,
Thus my dear Redeemer meet?
Not one day of service give Him,
Lay no trophy at His feet?
(Charles Carroll Luther, 1877)

Luke 19:10–27

"And as they heard these things, he added and spake a parable, because he was nigh to Jerusalem, and because they thought that the kingdom of God should immediately appear. He said therefore, A certain nobleman went into a far country to receive for himself a kingdom, and to return. And he called his ten servants, and delivered them ten pounds, and said unto them, Occupy till I come....And it came to pass, that when he was returned, having received the kingdom, then he commanded these servants to be called unto him, to whom he had given the

money, that he might know how much every man had gained by trading. Then came the first, saying, Lord, thy pound hath gained ten pounds. And he said unto him, Well, thou good servant: because thou hast been faithful in a very little, have thou authority over ten cities. And the second came, saying, Lord, thy pound hath gained five pounds. And he said likewise to him, Be thou also over five cities. And another came, saying, Lord, behold, here is thy pound, which I have kept laid up in a napkin: For I feared thee, because thou art an austere man: thou takest up that thou layedst not down, and reapest that thou didst not sow. And he saith unto him, Out of thine own mouth will I judge thee, thou wicked servant. Thou knewest that I was an austere man, taking up that I laid not down, and reaping that I did not sow: Wherefore then gavest not thou my money into the bank, that at my coming I might have required mine own with usury? And he said unto them that stood by, Take from him the pound, and give it to him that hath ten pounds. (And they said unto him, Lord, he hath ten pounds.) For I say unto you, That unto every one which hath shall be given; and from him that hath not, even that he hath shall be taken away *from him."*

First, he that earns the most gets the most rewards. In the parable, the one who earned ten pounds received ten cities to rule over, the one who earned five received five cities, and the one who did not earn anything received nothing. God does not divide up all the rewards equally—you get what you work for.

Second, praise can be a part of the reward. Even the second servant, who earned five cities, was not praised like the first, *"Well done, thou good servant."* I used to love to get praise from my dad. It made me happy to see how pleased he was with what I had done. I would sometimes do an extra-special good job just to impress him.

Also, notice the order of these servants is what you would expect. He that did the most was first in line, and he that did nothing was last. Those who are doing their best for our Lord are hoping He comes back today, and those who are not doing what God wants, hope His return is far off.

Thirdly, rewards are based on faithfulness: *"because thou hast been faithful."* Anyone can be a quitter! You want to hurt God's work? Just quit. Surely you can find a good excuse to quit: Someone was rude to you, your efforts are not appreciated, or others are exalted and received the position you deserved or expected. In this life, I have stood up front and received praise while my wife stayed in the background. But she and God know that I could not have done it without her. One time while Nancy was doing an undesirable job no one else would volunteer for, I asked her what she was thinking about. Her reply, "I was thinking that if Christ came back now, He would find me serving Him." What will keep you faithful in the hard times (I John 2:28)?

Fourthly, we are rewarded even for *"very little"* things. It seems like ever since I was in the military, it's been my job to pick up papers and trash off of the ground. My pastor asked me once to come down early and gather up trash at the church, and he wanted me to do it on a regular basis. I asked if there was not something else I could do, and he responded, "Brother, it's either you or me, and I'd rather it be you." When I became a pastor, I trained our people to pick up paper. I even showed them how to do it. But on Sunday morning, it was as though I was the only one who could see the paper on the ground. You might think that's a little thing, and actually it is, but God rewards for *"very little"* (Luke 19:17).

Want to try something a little harder? Serve as a nursery worker. Our ladies will come to church, sometimes forgetting it's their turn in the nursery, receive a tap on the shoulder, and hear, "You've got the dirty duty." Off she goes to change smelly diapers with crying babies, and one that will burp on her new dress. After the service, a mom will get upset with the worker because she forgot to change her baby's diaper. Of course, this worker is not receiving any pay for this, and she is beginning to wonder if even our Lord could put up with such.

The only time I made the honor roll was in the seventh grade.

The reason I never did before or after is because I wasn't interested in it. If you say I should have been, you're right, but then I didn't care. All I wanted was just to get through school. My older sister, on the other hand, always made the honor roll, and she loved to show Dad her report card. This usually got me into trouble because my report card came out at the same time as my sister's, and Dad would say, "Son, where is yours?" Then I had to find my report card and show him, while my sister stood behind and listened as I was rebuked.

What motivated me to make the honor roll, that one time in seventh grade, were two girls who had made fun of my grades. They had made the honor roll for the semester and were congratulating each other when I decided I would join the conversation. I said, "I could make the honor roll if I wanted. All you've got to do is study." They stopped and stared at me and then just laughed out loud and walked off! I thought, "They really think I'm stupid." I decided this once I would do my best and make the honor roll!

That next semester, on my first test I got a *B*, which really bothered me because I thought, with all the effort I put in, I would surely have earned an *A+*. Then a terrifying thought came over me: "Maybe I really can't do this!" I'm glad on my second test I merited an *A*; otherwise, I might have given up.

I had to move away from my friends and sit up front in the class because my buddies would cut up, and I could not listen. This brought me a little persecution. "You trying to be teacher's pet? You think you're better than we are, don't you?" Actually, it was "no" to both questions. I just wanted to make the honor roll. The Bible tells us we are deceiving ourselves if we think our wrong friends will not affect our Christian life (I Corinthians 15:33).

When report cards came out, I already knew I would be on the honor roll because I had asked each teacher. My old friends had that sick look on their faces when they received their report cards, and I could not help but laugh; I knew that feeling well.

There were two things I did with my report card. First, I found those two girls who had laughed at me. I walked straight up to them and shoved my report card in their faces and said, "This is my report card!" They stared at my grades in disbelief, and then I laughed really loud and walked off. Second, I went home and waited for my dad, sitting outside on the front porch. My sister came home and wanted to know why I was waiting outside, and I said, "You'll find out." When Dad arrived home, I put my report card in his face and said, "Look, Dad!"

He put down his lunch pail and began to read my grades and then said, "I'm proud of you son!" And added, "I guess you will be getting grades like this from now on?" I just shrugged my shoulders. What's the point? Our report cards are coming up in Heaven. Some will get *"gold, silver, precious stones"* and others *"wood, hay, stubble"* (I Corinthians 3:12). What are you going to receive?

ADVENTURE #9

Ye have not, because ye ask not"
(James 4:2)

There are things God will not give us simply because we will not ask for them! For some, it's pride that keeps them from asking God. "I don't need anyone's help" is their attitude. There are some things you could have had already in your life, or some that God will never give you because you will not ask Him for them, so, *"Ye have not, because ye ask not."* (James 4:2) Why haven't you asked God? You don't want to get your heart right with God? You forgot? Lack of faith?

Many people get through life without God's help, but that's a low plan to live on! When we get to Heaven, the last thing I would want to hear is, "See all these things I wanted to give you while you were on earth, but you forgot to ask!" If I do not receive something from God, I don't want it to be because I didn't ask for it. Many people pray daily to God, praise Him, and pray for others, but forget to share with God what really is bothering them.

If God says *no* to your request, or *wait*, then praise Him anyway; but ask! There is a passage of scripture in Joshua 15:18–19, where Caleb's daughter had received some land from her father, but it was a dry land without water. She said, *"Give me a blessing; for thou hast given me a south land; give me also springs of water."* She was not afraid to ask. If you have the thought, "I should just be satisfied with what I have and not bother anyone," then you may end up with a south land with no water on it. True, this would be better than no land at all, but why not have both? Notice she did not ask for one spring but for *"springs,"* and her father gave her at least four (see verse 19). When she asked, she could have said, *"May I have a spring?"* But hey, if you're going to ask, then ask for *"springs"*!

If we are going to ask just for our own selfishness, then yes, that would be wrong (James 4:3). But there are gifts from God we could have already had, had we been willing to humble ourselves and ask Him.

Things you might ask God for include: joy, happiness, peace, a wife or husband, to be a better father or mother, wisdom to answer a question or solve a problem, power and grace to do what God wants, a job, etc.

Have you ever prayed for an hour? *"What, could ye not watch with me one hour? Watch and pray,..."* (Matthew 26:40–41). *"Casting all your care upon him; for he careth for you."* (I Peter 5:7). I would rather do spiritual battle in prayer for one hour on my knees than to worry about something for one week! *"Be careful for nothing; but in every thing by prayer and supplication with thanksgiving let your requests be made known unto God. And the peace of God, which passeth all understanding, shall keep your hearts and minds through Christ Jesus"* (Phil 4:6–7). Pray and ask God to give you peace that your problems will be resolved.

There are two parables where Christ teaches us that if we do not receive what we want, then keep praying (Luke 11:5–8, 18:1–5). Why? One would think, "If God wants me to have it, He will give it to me, and if not, then why should I keep asking Him for it?" Well for one thing, if we keep praying for something, eventually we will have to ask ourselves what our motive is; "Why do I really want this?" Or, God *may* want you to give up some things (I Samuel 1:10–17). *"Delight thyself in the LORD; and he will give thee the desires of thine heart."* (Psalm 37:4) What is the desire of your heart? If we go every day to the Lord in prayer for our heart's desire, eventually we will ask, "What is your will Lord?" And be willing to say, *"O my Father, if it be possible, let this cup pass from me: nevertheless not as I will, but as thou wilt."* (Matthew 26:39) Spending time with God is always good, I see myself more clearly (my needs) and God's will for my life better. Also, I am more thankful to Him for his patience and love for me.

If we keep praying, we will get close to God. *"Draw nigh to God, and He will draw nigh to you"* (James 4:8). Some of the problems and burdens we have were designed by God, not only to turn us to Him, but also to keep us where He wants us (II Corinthians 12:7–10). If we always get what we want the first time we ask, we make God into our own personal servant. And we also forget about Him just as fast, or until the next time we need His help; and we don't appreciate as much what He has done for us. I prayed for years that my dad and mom would be saved. How important is it to you to get your desire from God? A dream is a precious thing, and it is worth the extra effort to not only commit it to prayer, but also, if need be, fast for it. Fasting increases your power in prayer (I Corinthians 7:5, Mark 9:29). Thankfully, God oftentimes answers prayers immediately (Matthew 14:30-31).

One day, my pastor asked me to build a platform for the new electric organ the church had bought. Our Sunday services were in one building, but our midweek services were in another building across the street. To move the platform for the organ back and forth between the two buildings, we would need wheels on it. I told him I could build the platform, but if he wanted anything more than shopping cart wheels, I could not help. He assured me he had confidence that I could make some thick rubber wheels with bearings in them. And I assured him I couldn't. Making something out of wood was one thing, but metal supports for wheels and special bearings were, for me, an impossible dream. I looked all that week for the proper supplies in every hardware store I could think of, but to no avail. I might add, this was back in 1977. Had it been today, I could have found something appropriate.

I called my pastor the night before we had to have the platform and explained I would have the project finished before the new organ arrived, but I had found nothing except shopping cart wheels. He said, "Do something, because we need it tomorrow."

I prayed a short prayer that night and simply said, "Lord, I don't mind making this platform, but I don't want to make something that would be junk and wreck the new organ." That next morning I set out to look in one more store for some larger wheels. As I walked out the church gate, I was stopped by four boys, who ran right up alongside me, even blocking my exit. They were dragging four commercial casters attached to short wooden planks. The wheels were the type professional movers use. They were about ten inches tall and three inches wide, and they were made of soft rubber with ball bearings in both the wheels and on the metal supports.

I knew the boys from Sunday school and asked them, "Where did you get these?" They told me a truck had passed in front of the church and hit a bump in the road, and the wheels fell out the back! Now you know if I had been there to see that, I would have been a "nice guy" and tried to contact the driver and return the wheels. But God brought the wheels to His church. The Lord says if you *"forgot a sheaf in the field, thou shalt not go again to fetch it: it shall be for the stranger, for the widow: and for the fatherless"* (Deuteronomy 24:19).

I asked the boys, "Hey, can I have those? We need them for the church."

They responded, "Sure."

Later that day when the pastor came by and saw the new cart with the commercial wheels, he said, "I knew you could do it." And when he asked where I found the wheels, I said, "They fell out of a truck and landed in our driveway!"

It was special delivery, right to our gate, as I was passing through it. A minute later and I would have driven off in my car. It was better than I hoped for, and the price was right—free!

"And this is the confidence that we have in him, that, if we ask any thing according to his will, he heareth us: And if we know that he hear us, whatsoever we ask, we know that we have the petitions that we desired of him." (I John 5:14-15) *Pray!*

ADVENTURE #10

You are an original!

There is no one else in the world like you! There are no two snowflakes alike, and no two people alike. Even identical twins are different, if not on the outside, then on the inside. And everyone has different fingerprints. God made us all different, and God does not want you being someone else. *You are an original!*

Several years ago, I read in a newspaper about a young man who wanted to look like Michael Jackson. This young man already had certain facial similarities with the famous pop star, and his friends even told him he looked like Michael Jackson. But his nose was not exactly the same, so he asked his dad if he could have $5,000 to have plastic surgery for a nose job. His dad said no, and a few days later the young man killed himself. Regrettably, this is a true story.

When I was fifteen years old, my parents took me to the local Kmart to buy me a coat for winter. The coat they wanted and the coat I wanted were not at all the same. I had seen a teenager wearing a coat like the one I wanted, and for whatever reason, I thought it was "cool." I had a long face because I could not get the one I wanted. My dad saw this and, although he was upset with me, he went ahead and bought me both coats, something that financially was hard for him. Looking back now, I believe the one my parents picked out was nicer looking, and, oddly, the one I picked out I would not wear today. But then my head was "screwed on backward," so I walked around in an ugly coat, just because I thought it was cool.

Some years later, I heard a lesson by a Bible teacher about a poll that had been taken in Hollywood, asking movie stars if there was anything they would change about themselves if they could. Movie stars are looked upon as being the most beautiful, famous, and rich people. But according to this teacher, an astonishing 95 percent said they would change at least one thing about their appearance—the colors of their eyes, or hair, or height, body build, etc. This same teacher said, "If you could stand in front of a mirror and change one thing about your appearance, what would it be?" He then challenged us to thank God for this feature we did not like. *"In every thing give thanks: for this is the will of God in Christ Jesus concerning you"* (I Thessalonians 5:18).

I had size 11 shoes when I was in junior high school, and some girl in the hall between classes noticed my feet and said, "You have big feet!"

"No, I don't," I said.

"Yes, you do!" And then she asked me in front of others, "Can you walk on water?" I told her not to say that, and I walked off. When I got home, I said to my mom,

"I have big feet!"

"No you don't," she reassured me, and then she asked, "Who told you you've got big feet?"

"Everyone knows it." I said.

You will not believe what I did, and I am embarrassed to tell you, but for the next four years, I wore shoes that were too small for my feet. You might think that was really dumb. Actually, it is worse than dumb—*it is painful*! I had four operations on my two big toes because of ingrown toenails. Why in the world would I do this? Because a girl in seventh grade said I had big feet.

If 99 percent of the world had only one arm,

I am sure that rest of us "freaks" with two arms would wish we had been born with only one. *"[B]ut they measuring themselves by themselves, and comparing themselves among themselves, are not wise"* (II Corinthians 10:12).

There is no outward ideal, only an inward one of Christ in you (Galatians 4:19). God wants us to be thankful for who we are and how we look. God made no mistakes! I taught this in church, and one time, unexpectedly, a teenage boy blurted out, "Do I have to accept this?" And he pointed to the birthmark on his face. It was an awkward moment for me, for though I knew what the right answer was, I also knew I would not want his birthmark on my face.

I told him, "Yes, for that also." There are people with scars or who have been disfigured by fire, but *God has grace for this*. However, grace is not forced, we have to want His grace, we have to ask for it. (II Corinthians 12:7–10). King David said, *"For thou hast possessed my reins: thou hast covered me in my mother's womb. I will praise thee; for I am fearfully and wonderfully made"* (Psalm 139:13–14). Have you ever thanked or praised the Lord for making you and giving you the looks you have, especially that which you would like to change?

Have you ever seen an older person dress up as a teenager, trying to look younger? Silly, isn't it? Why be someone you're not? Be the person you were made to be. I will never forget a response I heard from a teenager to another teen, who had made fun of his face. The one had said to the other, "You got a baby face!" Whereupon the other teenager replied, "So?!" I really admired him for it, and the one who had criticized him had no response. We should never make fun of the appearance of others. *"Whoso mocketh the poor reproacheth his Maker"* (Proverbs 17:5, *"poor"* in any sense.). We need to accept ourselves and thank God for making us the way we are. *You are an original,* accept yourself!

I have three beautiful daughters. One has very curly hair, one has perfectly straight hair, and one has hair with natural, gentle curls. They all have beautiful hair! Because we are all different, what looks good on one will not look good on another. Well, my daughters, with their beautiful, natural hair, all changed their hairstyles when they grew older—but not as

"Daddy" would have liked. I asked the Lord to help them see what I thought I saw, and I remembered that when I was fifteen years old, I would not wear the nice coat my dad bought me.

One of the things I wish I could relive in my life was when I was that fifteen-year-old boy in Kmart with the long face. Now, I would gladly take that ugly coat I wanted and put it back and wear the nice coat my parents got me. I also would have thanked my dad for loving me enough to do the best he could. *"When I was a child, I spake as a child, I understood as a child, I thought as a child: but when I became a man, I put away childish things"* (I Corinthians 13:11).

Some young preacher boys try to be like some famous preacher, but all the apostles were different and God wants you to be also, thou still obeying His Word. How can anyone live the greatest adventure of all, *life*, trying to be someone else? *You are an original!*

BOOKS and SITES by G.M. Matheny

The Layman's Biblical Handbook. For *FREE*, this site covers more than 200 biblical subjects.
http://www.thelaymansbiblicalhandbook.com/
Besides English it is also in,
Spanish http://www.manualbiblico.com/
Romanian
http://www.471633614246918175.com

True Christian Short Stories. Read for *FREE*, and besides short stories, this site has books and videos by this author.
http://www.truechristianshortstoriesfreebygmmatheny.com/
Besides English, this site is also in,
Spanish, Pequeñas Historias Cristianas - Home
http://www.pequeashistoriascristianasporgmmatheny.com/
Romanian, Scurte Povestiri Creştine de G. M. Matheny
http://www.scurte-povestiri.com/
French, Petites Histoires Chrétiennes Vraies -

Books by GM Matheny

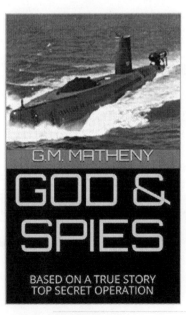

GOD & SPIES
BASED ON A TRUE STORY
TOP SECRET OPERATION

In Adventure #7, I gave the censured version of our Special Operation, but the CIA has now declassified this operation. Both eBook and paperback can be found on Amazon.com.

"Garry Matheny is a friend and a fellow preacher. Prior to his salvation he served in the US Navy as an elite saturation diver. He was involved in one of America's most important (and dangerous) clandestine operations.

"Garry does a marvelous job of weaving recently declassified information regarding the operation, the record of an intelligence analyst spending the rest of his life in prison for selling the details of this operation to the Russians and his own eyewitness account of the operation itself.

"If you like good old-fashioned American bravado, espionage and American history, you will enjoy this book."

Pastor Marvin McKenzie

Both paperback and Kindle.

https://www.amazon.com/dp/B07TCSLFWR

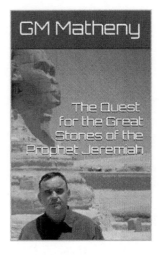

The Quest for the Great Stones of the Prophet Jeremiah.

The first in our Quest Series.

Stories about mystery or adventure have planted the thought that you have to be single and chasing your girlfriend to have any fun, and at the end of the story the couple embrace, kiss, and then on the screen or the printed page, appears "The End." The unspoken thought is, when you settle down and get married, the fun is over.

My wife, Nancy, our son Caleb, and myself, with Jesus Christ as our leader, made our own "special ops team," gathered "intelligence," and set off on an adventure of discovery! This took place between February 2005 and October 2008 and shows how Christians armed with the Bible found what the scholars could not.

What others are saying. "Garry Matheny

makes a terrific adventure story out of just two verses in the Old Testament book of Jeremiah. The amateur sleuth beats some of the world's top archaeologists at their own game, and you get to go along for the ride. You'll enjoy it!"

Both paperback and Kindle.

The Kindle edition is presently on sell for .99 cents!

https://www.amazon.com/dp/1981082832

Or read for *FREE*.

https://www.truechristianshortstoriesfreebygmma theny.com/the-quest-for-the-great-stones-of-the-prophet-jeremiah.html

The Quest for the Red Sea Crossing

The second in our Quest Series and should be read before our book *The Quest for Mount Sinai.*

Did the ancient Egyptians leave an account of the Red Sea

(Yam Suf) crossing? Most people who have studied this would respond, "But the ancient Egyptians never monumentalized their defeats." Yes, and today no one is expecting to find an ancient Egyptian inscription that says, "The God of the Hebrew slaves beat us up." However, there is an Egyptian legend (not the el-Arish Shrine) that does more than just lend itself to the sea crossing by Israel. It is about a battle between two Egyptian "gods," and in this battle, the "good god," who represents Egypt, loses (something very rare), and the "bad god," who represents the foreigners, wins, and it takes place at the bottom of the sea! And what is of more interest is that this takes place right in front of the four place names of the Red Sea/Yam Suf crossing, as given in Exodus 14:2! (Pi-hahiroth, Migdol, Baal-zephon, and "the sea.") But because this Egyptian legend was said to have happened in an unexpected location, it has been passed over.

Both paperback and Kindle.
The Kindle edition is presently on sell for .99

cents!

Or read for *FREE*

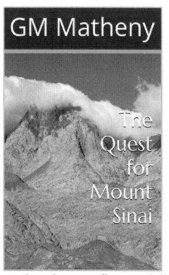

The Quest for Mount Sinai
The third in our Quest Series.

A pharaoh of Egypt went to Mount Sinai and engraved his named there! In December 2013, two years after our book was first published, an inscription made by a pharaoh of Egypt was found at the mountain that I have proposed as Mount Sinai. And more than a hundred years ago, a hieroglyphic inscription was found in the East Nile Delta, also made by a king of Egypt, describing an expedition to a location the scholars have hotly debated. But the location is now confirmed, for the same king made both inscriptions, and he found something there that Israel left at Mount Sinai.

Both paperback and Kindle.
The Kindle edition is presently on sell for .99 cents!

https://www.amazon.com/dp/1983006815
https://www.amazon.com/dp/B07DBF8TYV

Or read for *FREE*
https://www.truechristianshortstoriesfreebygm matheny.com/the-quest-for-mount-sinai.html

Made in the USA
Middletown, DE
21 September 2019